Library
Partnerships

Library Partnerships

MAKING CONNECTIONS
Between School and
Public Libraries

Tasha Squires

Information Today, Inc.
Medford, New Jersey

First Printing, 2009

Library Partnerships: Making Connections Between School and Public Libraries

Copyright © 2009 by Tasha Squires

Library of Congress Cataloging-in-Publication Data

Squires, Tasha, 1972-
    Library partnerships : making connections between school and public libraries / Tasha Squires.
        p. cm.
    Includes bibliographical references and index.
        ISBN 978-1-57387-362-8
1. Libraries and schools--United States. 2. Libraries and students--United States. 3. Library cooperation--United States. 4. Public libraries--United States.
5. School libraries--United States. I. Title
    Z718.S68 2009
    021.2'4--dc22

                                                                    2008051647

Printed and bound in the United States of America.

President and CEO: Thomas H. Hogan, Sr.
Editor-in-Chief and Publisher: John B. Bryans
Managing Editor: Amy M. Reeve
VP Graphics and Production: M. Heide Dengler
Book Designer: Kara Mia Jalkowski
Cover Designer: Lisa Boccadutre
Copyeditor: Beverly Michaels
Proofreader: Bonnie Freeman
Indexer: Beth Palmer

www.infotoday.com

To my father, the best librarian I've ever known, and to my mother, a better writer than I could ever dream of becoming. Much love.

Contents

Acknowledgments

First and foremost, I must thank my good friend (and editor) Rachel Singer Gordon, without whom this book would never have been written. She convinced me that I *could* write a book! Countless librarians across the country have my gratitude for their invaluable input and insight into school and public library collaborations and partnerships. Special thanks to Gail Bush for enthusiastically embracing the idea and being a sounding board early on in the project. Heartfelt appreciation goes to my wonderful husband, Kent, who simply said, "Of course you can do it," and who always asked my daily word count. Finally, to our daughter, Saffron: Honey, I'm thrilled that you kept to your nap schedule while I wrote at least *half* of the book and went happily off to preschool for the second part!

Foreword

At first people refuse to believe that a strange new thing can be done, then they begin to hope it can be done, then they see it can be done—then it is done and all the world wonders why it was not done centuries ago.

—Frances Hodgson Burnett[1]

Almost a century after Frances Hodgson Burnett wrote *The Secret Garden*, Tasha Squires helps us see that *it* can be done. Our lively conversations over coffee (scheduled around her daughter Saffron's naptime) elicited a mutual passion for librarian collaboration. We shared school and public library stories of partnership fits, starts, and successes. When library partnerships are born and nurtured between school and public librarians, programs flourish that serve young people in extraordinary ways. Generations mingle, artifacts are displayed, hot books are booktalked, summertime is reading time, and exhausted librarians are fulfilled.

When I worked as a curriculum librarian in a public suburban high school in the 1990s, our school library media program staff received the National School Library Media Program of the Year (1996) recognition from the American Association of School Librarians, a division of the American Library Association. One identified strength of our program was our collaborative and multifaceted relationship with the Des Plaines (IL) Public Library. The youth services public librarians came to the high school to demonstrate online databases, and we partnered on numerous grant proposals to serve adolescents, including a Literature for All of Us project that selected teens to participate in poetry writing workshops.

The most dramatic example of our school/public library partnership, though, took more than four years to develop and eventually let us provide public library services for students residing in a low-income area of the school district. One small segment of our student body lacked access to public libraries because the town in which those students resided chose not to fund library referenda. To make a long story short, the project outcome gave these students public library access through a village ordinance that reimbursed 75 percent of the annual library fee per family. The public library's director offered to pre-pay this 75 percent to the municipality so that families would not be responsible for providing the funds (few of these recently immigrated families had discretionary money in their household budgets). The school principal authorized the use of vending machine money from the student activities funds to provide the remaining 25 percent of the library fee. Most of the families impacted by this project were originally from countries that did not have public library systems, so the adults were unfamiliar with the library services available for their family members. These families were invited to the high school to hear about this community opportunity from the principal, and of the 74 families eligible, 51 families applied for public library cards for all their family members. Their high school students were no longer deprived of the resources to which all the other students had access. These partnerships may initially seem daunting, but once created they seem so obvious, serve so many, and are so worthwhile.

More recently my role as a school library graduate educator allows me to share this view of the importance of library partnerships with future school librarians. Panels of school and youth services library practitioners are more than willing to share their experiences with newcomers to our field, proclaiming that successful partnerships develop into collaborative relationships and grow into collegial friendships that not only enrich library services for youth but fulfill us as professionals.

Across the country, public youth services librarians and school librarians with Tasha Squires's enthusiasm and inclusive nature are reaching out to each other to serve young patrons. They are moving beyond a history of isolation to tell their own stories of partnership; it might start with a small idea that grows annually with new partners. There eventually comes a time when those who hear these stories cannot imagine "why it was not done centuries ago." Join author and librarian Tasha Squires and the countless others you will read about in *Library Partnerships* as you prepare to take your first steps to walk the road between libraries.

Gail Bush, PhD
Professor, Reading and Language Department
Director, Center for Teaching Through Children's Books
Director, School Library Program
National-Louis University, Chicago, Illinois

Endnote

1. Frances Hodgson Burnett, *The Secret Garden* (London: Heinemann, 1911).

Introduction

Collaboration. The very word sends some people's hearts soaring—while others feel as if they're having a heart attack. Partnerships can be a source of frustration unless both parties are fully committed to the process, which accounts for the groans heard around conference tables when the words *teamwork, collaboration,* or *partnership* are mentioned. Yet both school and public libraries expect some level of collaboration. School library media specialists are taught from the cradle that collaboration is the Holy Grail when it comes to working with fellow teachers. Public librarians are reminded of the word as they are roped into volunteering for committee after committee—for the good of their library. While we all know what collaboration is, and we know that we are all supposed to be doing it, we don't always find the time for the one type of collaboration that is most important for promoting literacy in the youth we serve: collaboration between school and public libraries. This is a disservice to the youth we worry about night and day, trying to find ways to increase their desire to read, learn, and grow, both within and outside our library walls.

This is such an obvious avenue for partnership that it is sometimes overlooked. After all, why *wouldn't* schools and public libraries, which serve the same clientele, work together to create a community of learners? Yet in library school, this topic rarely comes up during public library classes. Most students on the public library track take coursework on serving youth or adults, including children's literature, reference, and readers' advisory classes. School library media classes, when they do address collaboration, tend to focus solely on collaboration between school librarians and teachers. While there is no disputing the importance of the information covered in each of these courses of study, where do we ever learn how to partner with each other?

Once out of school, we settle into our respective roles as school library media specialists or public librarians and work to establish ourselves in our chosen fields. Many school library media specialists begin their careers as teachers and later come to see the library as a wonderful place to connect on a different and important level with students. Collaboration with other teachers therefore makes perfect sense to them, and such partnerships within schools are made easier by sheer proximity. School librarians often fail to realize the ways in which the public library could assist them in their work with teachers and students. They see little reason to go outside their walls to build partnerships and instead focus their time and energy on cultivating internal relationships.

While public librarians are perhaps more aware of how they might collaborate with a school library (if for no other reason than to use it as a venue for attracting students to their summer reading programs), they can find it daunting to approach a school without possessing knowledge of its policies and procedures. The effort it takes just to get a district, say, to approve posting flyers in the schools can discourage even the most determined person. Besides, the librarians who might look to the schools as partners in programs, collections, and services are often those who are already the busiest, planning storytimes, arranging preschool visits, and working the night shift. Their demanding schedules are less than conducive to building and maintaining an elaborate relationship with even one school, let alone multiple schools serving a wide range of students in age and ability. Is it any wonder that another collaboration is rarely first on the priority list?

While this book shows how school library media specialists and public librarians can create a mutually beneficial collaborative relationship, at times it does appear that the public library can provide more services and resources to the school library than the other way around. Public libraries traditionally have more funding, materials, and resources than the average school library media center. Yet the school library has something the public library does not: direct access to the student population. So even though public librarians may be able to offer more presentations and materials to a school library media center, the school library can deliver the population the public library is seeking to serve. Keep this mutual benefit in mind while reading the later chapters of this book, where more emphasis is given to what the public library can provide for the schools.

Extensive research shows that students who have access to strong libraries do better in all subjects; these findings cannot be ignored. Keith Curry Lance's groundbreaking *Impact of School Library Media Centers on*

Academic Achievement: 1993 Colorado Study provided a huge boost of support for school libraries. This study proved that thriving, well-developed school library media centers were the essential ingredient for raising students' academic levels, and these findings were replicated numerous times in other states around the country. Where school library media centers were important in the community, students did well academically.[1]

Still, some school library media centers struggle to become the hub of their school and need the support of their local public library. Shirley A. Fitzgibbons has written in depth about how these two types of libraries must work together, stating that "cooperation may be the only solution to providing adequately for the library needs of children and young adults."[2] She recommends ways school and public libraries can work together on the road to collaboration. Key to success is a community support system with common goals and visions and adequate staffing.[3] This is, of course, an ideal goal. We can hope that someday all institutions and administrators will discover that it is better to work together than apart. In the meantime, what can we as individuals do *now* to further learning and begin partnerships?

This book will answer this question, as well as others, such as:

- What is the most effective way to approach the other library?
- Who should be approached first?
- How can collaborative projects develop into productive long-term relationships?
- What resources can be appropriately shared?
- How can librarians maximize their available time to create a partnership that benefits both libraries?
- How should librarians present the possibility of collaboration to their administrations to maximize the chances of a positive reception?
- How can connections be established with the other library so that they will survive personnel changes?

In answering these questions, I'll suggest practical solutions to the problems, frustrations, and—at times—even disappointments that these types of partnerships can bring. At the same time, I'll try to keep the focus on the sense of excitement and fulfillment you can experience when working together to enrich the lives of young people in your community.

Countless librarians across the country have realized that a productive relationship with the library "across the way" would benefit the population they serve. These librarians have ventured into the world of collaboration knowing that a positive relationship will be fruitful for all involved. Some of their stories can be found within the pages of this book. To gain a broader understanding of working collaborations and partnerships, I contacted members of the LM_NET, YALSA-BK, YA-YAAC, and ISLMANET-L discussion lists and asked them to share their stories. Their insights and comments are featured throughout.

When I first began my career as a librarian, I had an interest in working in the schools, but no experience. I also had a scholarship obligation that required me to work for two years in a public library after completing my MLIS. I was lucky enough to land a position in a large public library system where working with area schools was encouraged. During my tenure as a public librarian, my love of the schools and their assortment of teachers and students grew, and I developed a true understanding of what it means to be a school library media specialist. As the years passed, I felt the lure of the schools pulling me more and more, until I realized that my heart truly lay in serving students and teachers on a daily basis. I returned to school and am now completing my certification as a school librarian.

Working in the public library, I saw time and again how connections with the school libraries were invaluable to both sides. Yet when I returned to graduate school to become a school library media specialist, I heard little mention of this important connection. Collaboration was stressed only in terms of creating partnerships with teachers and students. Thinking back to my earlier MLIS program, I could not recall much discussion there of partnering with other libraries. Clearly, there is a disconnect. I have seen firsthand how librarians are indeed working together, and their questions about how best to interact and connect crop up repeatedly on both public library and school library discussion lists. Understanding the culture and concerns of each library gave me the impetus to delve deeper into how to create lasting and meaningful collaborations.

Endnotes

1. Library Research Service, "School Library Impact Studies, 2007," www.lrs.org/impact.php (accessed July 4, 2007).
2. Shirley A. Fitzgibbons, "School and Public Library Relationships: Déjà Vu or New Beginnings," *Journal of Youth Services in Libraries* 14:3 (2001): 3.
3. Fitzgibbons, 6.

Chapter 1

Relationships Take Work

True collaboration is not spontaneous. It involves building a relationship—like a marriage, friendship or business partnership.
—Kathleen Baxter and Susan M. Haggberg[1]

Beginning a relationship with another library and opening yourself and your institution to all its wonders and pitfalls may initially seem daunting. While research supports the importance of collaboration between libraries, it falls to *people* to create, maintain, and develop these relationships over time. Creating a bond with another library—with another person—takes time, and in some cases, a good deal of patience. As in any relationship, someone must make the first move and wait to see whether the overture will be returned or rebuffed. Successful first moves can be broken down into specific actions, and crafting a link with another library is no different. While building a partnership with a fellow librarian should be less difficult than creating a profile on Match.com, it still helps to be prepared. Knowing ahead of time what you want, and what you are willing to give, will assist you in launching a productive collaboration.

Establishing a Connection

You decide it would be a good idea to form a relationship with another library. The question then becomes, how should you begin this process? Many factors enter into the answer to this basic query. One very fundamental concern is whether your administration will encourage or discourage a partnership. After all, without their backing, your enterprise can go up in smoke very quickly. You may wish to test the waters by having an informal discussion with your administration before taking the time to create a more thorough presentation on the expected benefits of your endeavor. (Find some strategies to sell collaborative ventures to your administration in Chapter 9.)

Taking some basic beginning steps will increase your chances of success in dealing with the other library. As librarians know, the ability to ask the right questions lies at the heart of any reference interview; the same holds true when dealing with partnerships. Ask the following questions to ensure you start off on the right foot:

- Whom should I approach to initiate a collaborative partnership?

- When would be a good time to approach my colleague in the other library?

- What is the most effective manner of contacting the potential partner?

- What kind of assistance can I reasonably expect from the other library?

- Where should we conduct our collaborative work?

Finding the One

When you have settled on a potential partner library, you need to determine the right person to approach at the other institution; nothing will happen until you reach out to create a link with someone. Your situation determines your choice of contact, so I'll talk about this first from the perspective of the public librarian, then from the viewpoint of a school librarian.

But That's Private!

While this book focuses mainly on the connections that can be developed between the public library and the public school library, you can enlist the same techniques and recommendations in public library/private school partnerships. Many private school libraries are woefully underfunded and rely on assistance and support from the public libraries in their area. In addition, private schools can be an extremely supportive demographic group for public library programs and activities.

It's natural to be apprehensive when moving out of your comfort zone to try something new and different. Public librarians might be especially hesitant to enter into partnership with librarians in a private school out of concerns about bringing in materials or promoting programs that do not mesh well with the goals of the school. Librarians in private schools might feel tentative about working with a public library, fearing that they will meet with resistance from public librarians who may not want to serve a private entity. Keep in mind, though: Libraries are libraries, whoever funds them, and you will find commonalities in any partnership.

Simply be forthright when working together; don't hesitate to state any concerns you might have regarding materials or programs.

Public librarians need to factor many considerations into their decision-making process. The relationship you establish with school libraries depends in part on the number of schools your library serves. If your public library district encompasses multiple elementary, middle, and high schools, it can be difficult to build a personal partnership with someone in each school. Start by focusing on the schools closest to your library to avoid becoming completely overwhelmed. In a rural setting, it can be more manageable to truly get to know the people in all the schools, simply because there are fewer schools to connect with.

Of course, which schools you choose to connect with also depends on the population you are trying to target. For instance, if you are a young adult librarian, you will probably focus on middle and high schools, and children's librarians will look to the elementary levels; the way in which your library and school districts divide students serves as the final determination. As a young adult librarian, I worked with sixth- to twelfth-grade students, but I spent nearly all my collaborative energy on the four middle schools in our district. While I maintained a presence in the high schools through regular letters to English and social studies teachers, I established a more personal partnership with teachers and school library media specialists in the middle schools. (And, within those middle schools, I further targeted English and social studies teachers with my booktalks rather than opening these up to all teachers.) Utilizing your time efficiently is important in creating a healthy relationship, which will be discussed later in this chapter.

It seems logical first to approach the school library media specialist in the school(s) you have chosen. Unfortunately, though, not all schools have a school librarian. You might encounter situations in which one school library media specialist serves an entire district, overseeing an aide in each school, or in which a school library media specialist divides her time between two (or more) buildings. Such situations limit the time school library media specialists have available to interact with a liaison from the public library. Worse still, there may be no one staffing the school library on a regular basis—or there *is* no school library. In some rural communities and lower socioeconomic areas, a school library is considered a luxury or is not deemed important enough to maintain.

The enrollment statistics of each school also come into play. In larger institutions, time constraints may limit the collaborative efforts the school library media specialists can undertake. On the other hand, one advantage of working with a large school is that each department usually has a chair (or head), who can be very helpful in distributing information to teachers in that area. An awareness of each school's environment will aid you in the long run, and the size of the school will also help you determine just what kind of collaboration you would like to offer.

What if your library has previously been in contact with the schools in your district, but things didn't work out? Sometimes links are established only to deteriorate over time, when people leave their positions or there is no longer a specific need. In this situation, it is important to know what happened and why the collaboration failed to succeed. Approach your new collaborative effort from another angle, to help alleviate concerns that an unpleasant history will repeat itself. Be leery if people tell you a certain school is "hopeless" or "unresponsive." People's perceptions can be inaccurate or colored by their own relationships, so try again if you believe in the possibility of a partnership.

In some larger public library districts, there is a school liaison or coordinator who works cooperatively with the schools—an optimal situation.[2] If your public library district has such a position, utilize this person to the fullest. (If you *are* this person, use the following chapters to help you in your cooperative efforts.) If you work at a branch, find out whether someone in another building is currently building partnerships with schools before beginning your efforts. Do your homework!

Consult your own and other departments to help paint a clear picture of the services your library already provides to local schools and to get information on the connections already established. For instance:

- Many libraries offer cards to teachers and school library media specialists working at schools within their service area, even if they are not residents. Check with your circulation department to see if they already have a contact at the school(s) and a list of all the teachers.

- Some libraries have a bookmobile service. Does your bookmobile stop at any schools in the district? Ask bookmobile staffers who they communicate with to set up schedules for stops.

- A library's children's department often has established contacts with local schools. If you are a young adult librarian working under an adult or reference department, be sure to ask so that you complement their services rather than duplicating them.

Avoid stepping on others' toes, and honor existing contacts and partnerships. If your library turns out already to be actively engaged in some type of collaboration with the schools, see how you can assist with or expand on services already in place.

In general, if a school has a library media specialist, she is your first point of contact. Only once that relationship has been established should you begin communicating with teachers and other staff members. If no school library media specialist is available, turn to the teachers themselves or to their department heads (if these positions exist).

On the flip side, if you are a school library media specialist, you may have no idea whom to approach first at the public library—and with good reason. Unless you have had public library experience before moving to the schools, it's not readily apparent how library departments are arranged and who is in charge of what. Ponder the following points before deciding whom to contact at the public library.

Even the smallest town usually has a public library to serve the community. This is a wonderful testament to the fact that libraries are a vital part of society. However, particularly in rural areas, these libraries may be woefully understaffed and underfunded. If the public library in your area is extremely small and open only a handful of hours, or if there is no public library nearby, a meaningful partnership simply may not be possible. In situations such as this, school librarians should consider reaching out to their community college library instead. In sparsely populated regions, the community college library often acts as the de facto public library for the towns from which it draws students.

After identifying a public library to contact, look at the size of the population it serves. A quick look at its web page may give you an indication; larger libraries usually have a page specifying the populations they are actively addressing. (If not, check out State Public Library Statistics at www.lrs.org/public/other.php). Most libraries will have at least an adult/reference department and a youth services department that directly serve the public; some larger districts will break these down further into areas such as computer services, readers' advisory, young adults, and outreach. Once you know the various areas the public library allocates resources to, you can better target the right department to contact.

In a small town, it is fairly clear what area the local public library serves. In larger cities and suburbs, though, it can be confusing trying to determine which library covers what territory. A district library may cover two or more towns yet not serve all the students who attend schools inside those boundaries. Some schools may include students from three or more towns—and library district lines do not necessarily follow town and city boundaries, which can complicate the issue further. Larger cities may have a library system that includes a large main library and many neighborhood branch libraries, which offer programs, materials, and outreach. Before launching any partnerships, you need to know which public library or libraries are responsible for the needs of the students in your school(s). It makes little sense to pick a public library that can offer services to only a small portion of your student population.

As mentioned earlier, some public libraries designate one person to work with schools. If the library serves many schools, this liaison might be overwhelmed and eager to find partners who are willing to work proactively with him. Ask the liaison if there are other departments or librarians in the institution who might want to collaborate on better serving students and teachers.

Check with teachers in your building to see if they have had experiences with the public library; often teachers will reach out on their own. As former youth services librarian Jennifer Bromann writes of her own experience: "The idea for a booktalk began when the chair of the high school's English department approached our library, seeking help for 'Readers Are Leaders,' a program that encourages students to read nonassigned books, one day a week, during homeroom."[3] Teachers often live in the community in which they work, so some may already be regular public library patrons who have developed a friendly relationship with staff members. Solicit their advice on who may be receptive to your offer of collaboration. This gives you invaluable firsthand knowledge and also creates another layer of connection with those teachers.

In many larger districts, school library media specialists share information with their colleagues at monthly meetings. This is a perfect time to ask colleagues about their experiences with the public library. Some fellow librarians may already have reached out—ask who they contacted and whether their attempt was successful. Let's say you work in a middle school and find that the librarian from an elementary school in your district is holding a successful Battle of the Books in collaboration with the children's department at the public library. You may have quite a different project in mind, but the fact that the library already has an established link with a school is a good sign and offers a relationship you can build on.

Find out if the public library offers any special advantages for school staff, such as teacher/librarian cards that enable school employees living outside the public library boundaries to receive the same (or extra) benefits as regular patrons. Some public libraries will also set aside materials on a given subject for particular classes or place books on reserve for in-library use only. Being aware of current services at the public library will help narrow your search for a willing partner and will keep you from duplicating existing efforts.

If you work in an elementary school, begin your partnership quest at the public library's youth services department. If you work in a middle or high school, check with the youth services department and ask if it has a young adult librarian or other staff member who works with teenagers. You might also spend much of your time working with the adult reference staff, as they are more likely to have a collection of materials that meets the needs of your students and teachers. Get all the information you can about the structure of the library and where it spends time and money.

While this book focuses mainly on interactions between librarians, collaboration can occur between any number of individuals. For example, a public librarian might work extensively with a principal, or a teacher might want to do a project with the public librarian. One young adult librarian from Illinois has done projects both with the school library media specialist and with teachers in her local school. And a school librarian might work with five different people from the public library—simply because each has a specific area of expertise. This might be especially true when working in partnership on grants or larger communitywide collaborations. Public librarians should also keep in mind that not everyone staffing a school library media center will have completed a certification program. A school library may be staffed by a teacher who was asked to start working as the school librarian, by an aide, or by a PTA mom who turned a volunteer situation into a full-time position. Just because people do not have a certificate does not mean they are not fulfilling their assigned role; working together will help both of you grow and learn.

It's All About the Timing

When I worked as a young adult librarian, there were some days I dreaded going to the mailroom. It never failed: On the days I was busiest, racing around to finish the 15 things in my planner, my director would ambush me there. She had fantastic ideas for collaborative projects with everyone from the historical society to the gardening club. While I respected our director and valued her opinions, her timing always seemed to be off, and her collaborative spirit wired into the mailroom. This, inevitably, is where she would suggest her newest plan, as I tried to show interest while backing out the door to return to my list.

As we all know, if the timing isn't right, it isn't going to happen. Period. An awareness of your partner library's calendar is important to establishing a working relationship. Working with someone in another building whom you seldom see will create enough stress; pay attention to timing to minimize additional stress and problems.

Basic timing issues stem from the differing schedules of different types of libraries. School librarians need to remember that many public libraries are open seven days a week and stay open until 9:00 PM or later at least one night a week, depending on their staffing levels and the population they serve. Some close on Sundays during the summer, while others will remain open. Many staff members work at least some night hours (in most public libraries), along with regular or rotating weekend shifts. Knowing the work schedule of the person you are collaborating with helps alleviate frustration if she fails to return calls and emails quickly. You can meet with a public librarian after school or even on the weekend. Once you have identified a contact at the public library, find out her typical schedule and work with it as best you can.

Public librarians should understand that school libraries are open when their schools are, and some are also open for limited hours before and after school to accommodate students who walk to school or who lack access to a public library close to home. Many schools, especially high schools, are realizing the benefits of allowing students access to their library even when school isn't in session. Students can use library materials for recreational reading, work on homework assignments, and get help with research. The larger the school, the more likely it is to have extended hours during which you may be able to reach the school library media specialist or a library aide. On the other hand, in rural areas, where most students are bussed, not many school libraries remain open after hours. Make a quick phone call to the school office to determine the school library's hours and when it is staffed. Also check to see when the school library media specialist is present, in case he splits duties between schools.

Timing also becomes an issue with regard to large events, such as the summer reading programs in many public libraries. Summer reading creates a frenzy of activity and energy, often beginning as early as January, when initial plans are being made and contracts drawn up. Summer reading collaborations will be covered thoroughly in Chapter 3, but these programs also come into play in terms of timing for other projects. The end of the school year is generally a bad time to approach youth services librarians in public libraries about a project you are considering for the fall. They are typically in over their heads at this time of year, so the idea of planning anything new is beyond their capabilities. A particularly brave soul may sit down and give you an hour of her time—but chances are this person is an adult reference librarian! Summer *can* be a good time to talk to people in the reference department, to ask questions about the materials available for students, to ask about database classes, and to get a general feel for what the public library has to offer. Just don't be disappointed if your attempts at a partnership are brushed off during summer reading. Most likely this is not a case of your colleagues' not wanting to engage with you; it's a question of their not being able to *at that time.*

Similarly, a public librarian should not decide to contact a school library media specialist at the beginning of May and expect a speedy reply. Most school librarians are responsible for conducting inventories, not only of their books, supplies, and computers, but also of all of the school's textbooks—and, in some cases, all of the school's supplies, from desks to software. This process often involves closing down their library to inventory its contents, creating reports for their administration, and tracking down overdue or lost books, leaving little or no time to discuss possible partnerships. During May, the public librarian can offer to help by promoting her summer reading program at the school, but it is best to have this arrangement in place ahead of time.

While the beginning of the school year can be stressful for both school and public librarians—arguably more so for the school library media specialist—this is also a time when people tend to be fresh and optimistic. Public librarians have a successful summer reading program behind them, and school library media specialists have had time to recover from the previous school year. This is a good time to seize the day and initiate contact with your counterpart. A collaboration at the beginning of the school year can set a positive tone for the entire year, and everyone has a clean slate with which to start.

Making Contact

In our age of technological overload, simply deciding on the most appropriate way to initiate contact can be overwhelming. Of course, you already will have sussed out whom to approach and the best time to make contact. Now you need to determine which form of communication works best for both you and your recipient. Make sure to consider your own preferences—don't email someone if you never check your email, even if she prefers this form of communication. There are plenty of alternative avenues for contact.

The most immediate choice for your primary communication tool is likely to be email. Most librarians have an email account that they use on a regular basis. However, just because a school district or public library provides its employees with email accounts does not mean that they actually check their accounts. First, find out if your contact has an email account specifically for professional use. Then, find out if she actually uses and regularly checks this email—which can be a bit difficult. Wait a few days for a reply to your initial contact; don't assume she's uninterested in what you have to say. Send a follow-up email message, and if you still receive no reply, move on to another method.

The telephone is another powerful tool and can lead to some wonderfully spontaneous collaborative moments. When people begin to share stories and situations on the phone, the wheels get turning, and problems can be solved in minutes. However, many people prefer email precisely because of the immediacy of telephone communication. We all have used the expression "phone tag," and we despair when we need to have an answer quickly. Even worse is when you find you must rely on a third party to relay an important message. As with email, check to see if your contact has personal voicemail. Public librarians contacting school library media specialists should know that they may not have regular access to their voicemail; some schools have a single phone from which all staff must retrieve messages. However, because of the nature of library work, the school library often has its own telephone; the librarian frequently needs to place book orders and request repairs. Public libraries may not have a voicemail system, so school librarians may have to rely on leaving a message and hoping it reaches their contact. Knowing the other person's schedule and typical work hours is even more important when you are trying to connect by telephone. Remember, too, that because you are just beginning a relationship, it will take some time to establish a connection.

The good old U.S. Postal Service might be the best option for initial contact. With this method, the receiver has time to review material at leisure and can take time to reflect seriously on the possibility of an alliance; no one is waiting by the phone or computer for a return message. Sending out targeted mailings can also help establish a relationship without any expectations. As a young adult librarian, I created a monthly newsletter detailing young adult and adult programs and noteworthy items added to the collection. This publication was distributed in-house to our patrons, but I also included it in packets sent to each middle and high school in our district. I added memos addressed to the English and social studies teachers and the school library media specialists, listing events they might want to share with their students, services I could provide to the school, and materials the public library had ready for them to use. At the end of each letter, I specifically invited teachers and school librarians to contact me with any questions or concerns and included my work number and email address.

I cannot say I spoke personally to all of these teachers during my tenure at the public library. Yet teachers and school librarians would reach out to me when they had a need—simply because I had already established a communication route. My faithful correspondence showed my interest in assisting them with their work. Using this basic form of communication, I was able to reach several hundred people each month throughout the school year.

Consider sending a quick email or snail mail note each month to the person you would like to collaborate with. Let him know about the projects you have planned. Ask for his advice, or just keep him informed. The more information each library has about the other, the better your channels of communication. Make these notes a regular part of your monthly routine, and before you know it, you will establish a working relationship that's conducive to more elaborate collaborative projects.

You have probably already used one or more of these conventional methods to some extent to communicate with another library. If you just want to see whether anyone is interested in working with you, trying different avenues may help. Use other technological methods to make contact, such as becoming active on lists where school library media specialists and public librarians post and interact, such as LM_NET and YALSA-BK. Try starting a website or wiki for your library or department, and see what happens. Many public libraries maintain MySpace pages where youth and other librarians can interact with them. Create your own podcast or blog with information about books, materials, and concerns. Invite comments—you may be surprised by the number of people out in cyberspace who are listening to what you have to say. Use a website like evite (www.evite.com) to send out invitations to a special tea for all the school library media specialists in your public library district, or invite local public librarians in to see your library media center. The web offers so many possibilities for meeting and interacting with colleagues. (Detailed information on using technology in collaboration and partnerships can be found in Chapter 6.)

Realistic Expectations

Just as on a first date it is wise to avoid discussions of religion, politics, or when you'd like to get married, it is prudent to approach any new possible partnership with minimal expectations. While you may see a great variety of ways to work with another librarian, start by letting her talk about the types of partnerships and assistance she actually needs. A public librarian may be prepared to booktalk seven days a week (forgetting schools are only in session five), while the school library media specialist may have no current need for booktalks but instead needs a better understanding of how to request ILL materials. Try not to assume that what you want to offer is what the other library desires.

If you are a public librarian and are establishing contact with a school library media specialist or other school representative, start out on a positive note by asking about the kinds of services the school library currently offers its students. Be specific, so you get a better grasp of what resources the school has access to and what its needs may be. Learn about the cultural makeup of the school, as well as the socioeconomic background of its students. You may already have an idea, since these are the same youth who come to the public library. However, if your library serves a large community, or is in a remote location where transportation becomes an issue, you might not have this pertinent information. Next, ask what the school library may be lacking that the school library media specialist would like to change. It is important first to get a handle on your potential partner's perspective and needs, in order to build a relationship based on mutual assistance. Typically, getting this information will not be hard. Most librarians dream of what their library would look like without budgetary, administrative, and space restrictions.

School librarians might find approaching their local public librarians a more difficult proposition, if they are thinking only in terms of what the school library can offer the public library. It is important to find out what services the library currently

What Should We Talk About?

Here are some general questions to help you identify the other library's needs.

Questions a public librarian can ask a school library media specialist:

- How many students do you see in a typical day?
- What variation do you see in reading abilities among students in your building?
- Do you see many students with learning disabilities?
- What is your library's most pressing need in terms of materials/books/technology?
- What kind of budget do you have to work with?
- What kind of staffing do you have?
- What hours is your library open?
- Are there services you would like to implement but are unable to because of limited time/money/space/ cooperation?

Questions a school library media specialist can ask a public librarian:

- What hours/days are most popular for children and teens to visit the public library?
- Is there a designated area for children? For teens?
- How many programs are offered for children in a typical month? For teens?
- What kinds of programs do you offer young people?
- How do you promote your programs?
- Can students get their own library card? Are there any restrictions?
- Do you have computers for student use?
- Do you subscribe to any databases targeted for student homework help or assignments?
- Are there any discipline problems with children/teens in the library?

offers children and teens and what else the public librarian would like to provide. Keep in mind that the public library is run by numbers: tax numbers and budget numbers, but also numbers of materials circulated, numbers of program attendees, numbers of programs offered, and numbers of card holders. If you can assist in increasing any of these numbers, you will earn the eternal gratitude of the public librarian. Remember that you have a captive audience: Students regularly come into the school library for scheduled instruction or library periods, whereas public librarians must wait for children and teens to decide to come to them. By understanding this basic premise, you can figure out ways to assist each other.

In the end, it is important to be aware of the time you can realistically devote to collaboration and try not to exceed that limit in the early stages of your partnership. You can easily be swept away in the euphoria of finding someone else with plans—someone who actually wants to do something about them. Until you have established a good working relationship, be wary of investing too much energy in any one project. Maintain realistic expectations of each other; build slowly and progressively.

Your Place or Mine?

The time will come when phone calls, emails, and list postings are not enough. Or perhaps you both agree it would be better to meet in person to get things started. You might begin with just a friendly meeting, without any grand collaboration agenda. In fact, this is how some partnerships are set in motion—as was the case with two librarians from Anoka County, Minnesota. "It was just a get-to-know-you lunch. Yet unbeknownst to us, as we sipped soup and ordered sandwiches, we were laying the groundwork for a long, fruitful partnership."[4] Sometimes personal friendships lead to the first steps of collaboration.

If you are the one who initiated the conversation about collaboration, be willing to go to the other person's institution to meet face-to-face. You may have to give up your own free time. For example, on the way home from school, a school library media specialist might stop in to visit a public librarian, or a public librarian might visit the school librarian before work. These are trade-offs; you don't always need to meet at the other library, but be willing to make the extra effort to get the ball rolling.

How often you meet, and under what circumstances, depends on your situation and schedule. It is always fun to get out of the office routine and meet for lunch or coffee at a restaurant, as the Anoka County librarians did. Sometimes it is beneficial to see the space in which the other librarian serves children and teens. If you are invited to join a regular staff meeting at the other library, you will have a chance to meet other librarians and staff who may impact your collaborative efforts. Any chance you have to be present at an internal meeting at the other library will be extremely instructive for everyone.

Always respect the other person's time, and go into each meeting with a plan for what you want to accomplish. Be open to establishing a personal friendship with the other librarian; this makes working together more satisfying in the long run.

Rejection

We have all felt the sting of putting ourselves "out there" in our personal or professional lives, only to have our efforts rejected. This can be a disheartening experience, and you may feel so despondent as to think there is no reason to try again. (Of course, this reaction will likely pass as time goes on!)

Remember that when you approach people about collaboration, they bring all their own past experiences to the table, both positive and negative. You have no control over what has happened in their past and can only reassure them by pointing out the differences in this situation. Even so, realize that some people will not be enthusiastic about working collaboratively, and you must be prepared for the possible failure of your attempts to reach out.

Is My Email Working?

This is probably the worst-case scenario: You sent out your hopeful email, then sent a postcard, left a friendly letter in a mailbox, and even left a phone message (or two, or three, or four ...). Okay, so you've lost count of how many times and ways you have tried to connect with your contact at the other library. And nothing. No call, no bounced-back email, no returned letter saying "addressee unknown." What do you do if you get no response? Move on. Try not to dwell on it. Who knows, perhaps that person never figured out how to work the phone system, or the email, or the ... mailbox? In any case, if you have tried repeatedly to get in contact with someone, to no avail, it is probably safe to say she is not interested.

Learn from this experience. Go back and read over your messages: Were you asking what you could help with, or were you telling the other librarian what you thought she needed from you? Then, write it off as a learning experience. You can still try contacting this person on occasion in the future, but don't belabor the point. Instead, focus on whom you might contact instead. You might discover a willing partner in the reference librarian or the new social studies teacher. (And through your new contact, you just might wind up getting in touch with the person you were seeking to connect with in the first place.)

It's Not You, It's Me

An offer of collaboration may be met with wariness, skepticism, or even open hostility. This kind of response can throw you off base and leave you feeling unsure how to proceed. The person you contact may dismiss your idea with: "I've tried that, and it didn't work." End of story. In our profession, people sometimes stay in their positions for decades. Some may feel they have seen it all, or they may have been in their jobs for so long that they no longer have the energy or desire to try something inventive. Collaboration takes both time and motivation, and you may run into someone who is simply less enthusiastic about entering into a partnership.

While this can be frustrating, remember that you might have to deal with this person for a number of years. As a young adult librarian, I was able to begin working immediately with one school library media specialist, while it took me about four years to build a relationship with another one. Each person is different, and you must treat each with respect and an understanding of their position. Perhaps the children's librarian at your local public library has no interest in doing a presentation to your teachers about its databases. Or maybe the school library media specialist has no time to create a schedule for your booktalks. If they see that you are truly looking out for *their* best interests, as well as your own, they will be more willing to work with you in the future. A little goodwill goes a long way.

I'll Call You

Everything seems to be going along so well. You've made contact; the person was excited and ready to tackle all the collaborative projects you mentioned. She even offered some suggestions about when and where to get the ball rolling. So, smug and satisfied, you began plans for your grand joint adventure in serving your community's youth. But now, a week or two have gone by. Your deadline to chat has passed, and you've had no contact with your partner. In fact, you even left a few messages, with no response. This is puzzling because this person was so enthusiastic about your endeavors.

What could possibly have gone wrong? Frankly, it could have been anything. Did the person just feign enthusiasm to get you off the phone? Has he been preoccupied with something happening at his workplace? Did his supervisor change his duties? He may have been truly excited at first, but then the idea of all the work involved began to weigh heavily on his mind. Perhaps it was too much, too soon. In this case, the best thing to do is lay low for a bit. And when you do resurface, do not mention how you were let down. Offer to help the other librarian with a project or just to meet to chat over coffee. Sometimes just removing expectations can be a relief and allow you to proceed toward a collaborative partnership.

Courting Time—Learning the Art of Wooing!

If you encounter someone who seems to have been burned by the collaboration process one too many times, you may consider just offering to assist. Helping another person out now might just help you in the long run.

A school library media specialist can:

- Ask for copies of flyers about upcoming programs to post in the school library.
- Offer space to publicize library activities in the school newspaper/newsletter.
- Discuss how the school can help with discipline problems at the public library.
- Encourage teachers to accept extra credit for student attendance at public library programs.
- Alert the public library of any major school projects on the horizon.
- Put in an appearance at the public library board meeting and talk about how helpful their staff is to the school(s).

A public librarian can:

- Volunteer to help catalog/shelve/process/weed materials if the school library is understaffed.
- Call weekly or monthly to see if students are undertaking any large projects for which materials should be set aside.
- Offer assistance at book fairs, reading nights, and curriculum nights.
- Provide information on relevant databases students can access, either remotely or on-site.
- Speak at a school board meeting on the importance to the community of having strong school libraries.

Starting Over

It can be difficult to find that something you spent so much time researching and developing can fizzle—or never take shape in the first place. This, though, is all part of the process of creating partnerships. Realize from the start that not all collaborative situations will be fruitful or will meet your expectations. In any case, you learn something with each effort. Once the dust has settled, it is time to venture forth once again. Don't become reluctant to reach out.

Remember, work on your relationships with other people by finding out where they need assistance. Learn the operating culture of their library, find out whom to talk to, and know their schedules. Establishing collaborative relationships that enable you to expand your services to youth will take time and effort on everyone's part.

Endnotes

1. Kathleen Baxter and Susan M. Haggberg, "Ladies Who Lunch: Despite Their Minnesota Guilt, a School and Public Librarian Get to Know Each Other," *School Library Journal* 46:9 (2000): 33.
2. Jami Jones, "Come Together," *School Library Journal* 50:3 (2004): 45.
3. Jennifer Bromann, "The Toughest Audience on Earth," *School Library Journal* 45:10 (1999): 60.
4. Baxter and Haggberg, 33.

Chapter 2

Partnership Basics

On the road between friends' houses, grass does not grow. And neither should it grow between school and public libraries whether that road is paved or virtual.

—*Gail Bush*[1]

Wandering the labyrinth of partnership possibilities can be confusing. Searching for the right contact, making sure not to step on anyone's toes, and striving to assist dynamic populations all create anxiety. Partners should realize that the first tentative reaches toward each other need not be earth-shatteringly complex, nor must they demand a great deal of commitment. Know your limitations and your work environment before forming a cooperative or collaborative partnership; choosing to begin a massive project just weeks before your school lets out for the summer or just before the public library's summer reading program will set you both up for failure. Give yourself permission to start small and grow big.

The Basics

We constantly hear the old adages: take baby steps; eat an elephant one bite at a time; slow and steady wins the race … supply your own mythology here. The point is well taken, but it's easy to get frustrated when we see students who don't know how to use a basic software program, hear students moan about sustained silent reading, or (my personal favorite) encounter a student at the service desk who wants a book to answer a specific question his teacher has posed to the class—even though the answer is supposed be derived from his own thoughts and what he learned in class—and who can't understand why you can't supply the answer! We look at our students, the kids in summer reading and story-times, and despair of ever reaching enough of them to make a difference. As Abby Daniels, children's librarian at High Point Public Library in North Carolina, says, "I guess I'm on the right path—it's just a long, circuitous path, and I'm feeling impatient!" It's hard not to want instantaneous results, but the way to build productive relationships—with students or with other librarians—is one step at a time.

Once contact has been made, and you are fairly certain your prospective partner is actually reading your emails or enjoys receiving your newsletters, it's time to begin some small cooperative projects together. Preliminary projects usually last for a predetermined amount of time, are limited in scope, involve few people, and can be accomplished with a modicum of effort. These types of projects are an ideal way to get a basic cooperative relationship established between two libraries.

Quick and Easy

One easy way for public librarians to begin reaching students is by sharing what is happening in their libraries. When a young adult librarian plans a visit from a Civil War surgeon, complete with bloody limbs and hacksaws, it's a shame when only two adults show up (dressed in full combat fatigues!). This is not what the librarian had in mind. No doubt she was hoping that all those students who had come in requesting novels set during the Civil War would materialize to fill the seats. She assumed that they shared a profound love of the subject, when actually their interest lasted precisely as long as the mandatory assignment. (Of course, any teachers and school library media specialists reading this will be laughing!)

What was missing here? After all, presumably this public librarian posted flyers in the library, included information in the newsletter, and maybe even got a notice into the local newspaper (hence those two adults!). Those of us who have planned programs understand how difficult it is to predict which programs will succeed. In this case, though, since there was clearly a class assignment to study the Civil War, there should have been a ready supply of student attendees ... if extra credit had been offered. Aha! Yes, good old extra credit. It saved many programs for me (including one on the medicine of the Civil War). School library media specialists work with teachers all day long, know about assignments, and can see connections between the school curriculum and what is being offered at the public library. To complement the in-house resources available to students, school library media specialists should bring pertinent public library programs to the teachers' attention. Suggest that they offer extra credit for attending. This can be a win-win(-win!) situation. The public librarian has good numbers for her program, teachers are happy to see students engaged in the topic outside the classroom, and the school library media specialist can provide her students with more resources without spending a dime. Not to mention the obvious benefits students derive from expanding their knowledge base on a subject.

Public librarians should make it standard practice to supply the local school libraries with flyers or posters about pertinent programs and ask if they can be displayed prominently. School librarians should be on the lookout for public library programs that match the curriculum and alert teachers to possible connections. If teachers choose to offer extra credit, the school librarian can make a quick call to the public librarian and suggest that she print up attendance certificates for the students to take back.

School library media specialists also should not hesitate to suggest that the public library present programs targeting various areas of the curriculum. Most public librarians would be thrilled to plan a program they know will be well attended. For instance, a public library might not ordinarily schedule a Harriet Tubman storyteller in November for fear of poor attendance. However, if local fourth and eighth graders are all studying slavery in the fall, the library could feel confident scheduling such a program, so long as they get the word out in the schools. Schools are often limited by their budgets as to the types of programs they can provide, while many public libraries have budgets allocated specifically for such programming.

Of course, school library media specialists should feel free to ask public libraries to publicize their work as well. Perhaps you are holding a community open house or having a craft fair to benefit the school. Maybe the school science fair is open to the public, or you are looking to draw more people into your book fair. Never miss an opportunity to help each other and cross-promote your programs.

Meetings, Meetings, and More Meetings

As mentioned in Chapter 1, a good way to maintain contact with the other library is by attending its meetings. Ideas emerge in meetings, and golden opportunities abound—but you need to be present to take advantage of them. Sometimes, just your presence in the room will provoke comments and questions, even if you are ostensibly there as an observer. Getting invited to a meeting might require some finesse on your part; however, it will be worth your time. Your glimpse into the lives and concerns of your colleagues in other libraries lets you better understand their issues and facilitates meaningful communication.

While it is wonderful to attend one meeting at your partner library, it is even more beneficial if you can return. Many public libraries hold monthly department meetings, while school districts often have regular gatherings for all their librarians. While it is impossible to attend all of these meetings, try to make them regularly. Here are some issues to keep in mind when visiting another library for a meeting:

- Make sure supervisors are aware of and support your presence at any meeting. You don't want to get your colleague in trouble by coming to a "private" department meeting.

- Bring along any new informational brochures from your library, and always try to have some sort of handout so that when you leave, you'll be remembered.

- Try to learn everyone's name, position, and/or school. This is both common courtesy and an avenue to potential contacts.

- Remember, you are a guest, not the keynote speaker. Limit your input to your areas of expertise, and offer opinions only when asked.

- Once your presence is firmly established and accepted, ask if you can contribute agenda items in order to share information and introduce ideas for collaboration and cooperation.

If you are unable to attend, ask if you can see the meeting agenda, just to keep yourself informed. If you develop a relationship with the other librarian, ask if she can present an agenda item on your behalf and report the results.

School librarians should also realize that interest in the public library from other community entities strengthens its position in the eyes of both its board and the community. Another way to gain a snapshot of goings-on at the public library is by attending board meetings, which are open to the public. At some meetings, visitors are asked to state who they are, which gives you a chance to show that the schools are interested in the public library. Similarly, public librarians can attend a school board meeting, which provides an opportunity to show your interest in the school, and specifically the school library.

Attending meetings might not always be possible. School librarians might have union restrictions on their time or be committed to classes during the school day, while public librarians might not be able to get away during the rush of after-school youth to meet at a school. Still, consider this option as one way to build partnerships with the other library.

They're Coming!

One of the most frequent complaints from school *and* public librarians is the lack of notice teachers give regarding assignments. As retired Illinois school library media specialist Leslie Hrejas states: "The problem is that most teachers are not trained to *use* the library. They might run in and want something ... *now* ... but they don't realize that it will be a problem to assign every kid a project when there are only maybe 10 books on the subject in the library. I ran into this constantly. The second grade teacher would bring in her class for library time and ask me if I could please have each child check out a planet book, on their reading level! I was lucky to have 10 books on the planets, and they definitely were not all at a second grade reading level." Public librarians are forever reminding local schools to give them some type of warning as to when 500 sixth graders are about to descend, all asking for recipes from the Middle Ages. We all long for assignment alerts to be filled out in triplicate, signed, sealed, and delivered—preferably with at least a week's notice. We can dream!

Even though we know this is an impossible dream, what we hope for—and what an assignment alert can give us—is, of course, time to prepare the materials we have available, locate missing materials, and order new ones to fill in any gaps. One of my first duties as a new young adult librarian was to create an updated version of our public library's assignment alert form and publicize it like crazy. This effort met with little success. I was always shocked on the rare occasion when the old form showed up in the fax machine. Frankly, I thought everyone had thrown it out immediately. This is not to say that teachers don't care about letting you know what is coming, but they tend to be so busy that they simply forget. They may be in the process of working out a new curriculum standard, so they themselves don't know until the last minute what materials the students will need. With more current means of communication, the old assignment alert paper form has probably seen its best days come and go—and even its best days depended on teachers to be very savvy and organized.

Show You Care

Have you had difficulty getting the other library to respond to your pleas for help with school assignments? Try some of these ideas, and demonstrate your interest in working together.

Public librarians can:

- Be aware of new assignments. Ask coworkers what youth are asking for, and get copies of assignment sheets if possible.
- Pull books for assignments and reserve them for in-house use. Contact the school library media specialist and let him know you have books on hold for his students.
- Maintain a folder of repeat assignments. Pull books and other materials ahead of time to meet the demand— after checking to see if the assignment is still in this year's curriculum.
- Select new materials based on the previous year's assignments. Ask the school library media specialist for suggestions of specific purchases.
- Request copies of the school's textbooks for an in-library collection.
- Have the school curriculum standards available, as a personal reference and for collection development purposes.

School library media specialists can:

- Alert public librarians when a major project is approaching.
- Ask for certain materials to be reserved for in-house use. Provide specifics about the grade level and types of materials needed.

- Try to stay aware of projects for which the public library may not have materials, perhaps because the topics are not in line with the goals or vision of the public library. Try to steer teachers in a different direction with the assignment.
- Work with teachers to help determine what materials are needed and which of these are available from the public library.
- Go to the public library and work with the librarians to collect the materials needed.
- Attend a public library board meeting and mention how helpful the staff has been in assisting the schools.

Now, many librarians are taking matters into their own hands. As Linda Wunderlin, media specialist at New Haven Middle School in Indiana, says: "When we have a project topic going on, I send an email to my contact at the local public library. She puts together a collection, so that when the kids come looking, they are directed to the already pulled collection." This method cuts down on the possibility that there is no ink in the fax, that teachers forget to send an alert, or that an alert gets lost in someone's mailbox till the day of the assignment. There are many ways to work cooperatively on getting the appropriate materials into the hands of students; calling or emailing the public librarian can be the quickest and best. Some public libraries post assignment alert forms on their websites, which can be accessed by teachers or school library media specialists. (For a good example of an online alert form, see the Ramapo Catskill Library System's form at www.rcls.org/forms/wplaaform.html.) Working together to provide materials for students is a great way to begin a cooperative relationship.

Time for Tea?

It's common knowledge among young adult librarians: If you feed teens, they will come. If you provide food at any function or program—or just happen to be walking through the library with a plate of cookies—teenagers will magically appear. I will go on record in saying that adults are pretty much the same. When trying to get people into a public library to showcase the services you can provide, or just to be friendly, there is no better way than to invite them over for tea and cookies, or coffee and donuts, or bagels and cream cheese, or—well, you get the idea. Socializing and food have harmonized beautifully for years, so why break with tradition? Many public libraries have realized this is a great way to interact and connect with many people in a short amount of time. Of course, preparation for the event will take some work. However, the chance to inform the schools about the library's services and to make connections is worth the effort. Sandy Moltz, of Swampscott Public Library in Massachusetts, says that traditionally "the middle school and high school librarians try to do a dinner out with me and my library's director once a year. It gives us a chance to socialize and talk about what's happening at our respective institutions. In fact, this past year we included all the town's school librarians (elementary level, too). As of now, the layoffs in our town are so severe that the current high school and middle school librarians may both be gone and replaced by bumping one of the elementary school librarians. So, I'd say that it's serendipitous that we included all the librarians at our last dinner."

Public librarians are not the only ones having guests over for snacks and a good chat; school librarians are realizing the practicality of holding these events for their fellow librarians as well. Invite the youth services staff, as well as the public library's director and perhaps some of the reference staff. This will go a long way toward expanding their understanding of the limitations placed on school libraries. If the public library director sees for himself that your whole 900s section only takes up two shelves, his eyes will be opened. He might have more consideration for students' requirements and what the public library can provide.

If you decide to invite guests into your library for the purpose of creating common understanding, keep the following in mind:

- There is no such thing as too much planning. Know what your goals are for the get-together, and keep them front and center throughout the planning process. Is this a time to highlight new additions to the collection, focus on ways to connect better with each other, or discuss resource sharing?

- Timing is always an issue. Typically, though, just before the beginning of the school year is a good time to approach participants, from either the public library or the schools.

- When creating your guest list, make sure not to leave out anyone vital, such as the library director or school principal.

- Real invitations (paper or electronic) always lend a nice touch. Be clear about RSVPs.

- Try to involve as many of your staff and colleagues as possible. The more participation from your own building, the more support you will have for future collaborative efforts.

- Leave time for people to mingle and gather refreshments before beginning a presentation.

- Make sure your presentation is pertinent to the group you have assembled, and build in time for discussion of the topics you want to address.

- Always have a handout that includes important agenda points, presenter names, and contact information.

- Enjoy your time with fellow librarians and other people who have dedicated their lives to working with youth!

It is fun to bring others onto your home turf and show them what you do there, so take this opportunity to show off a bit. Encourage dialogue among all the participants, and do not be surprised if this simple get-together facilitates your first real collaboration with the other library.

Who Wants to Be a Librarian? Anyone?

A school library media specialist once invited me to present at an eighth-grade Career Day. In keeping with the spirit of building our relationship, I accepted. Of course, I was thrilled and eager to spread the gospel of librarianship. I tried to be peppy—and even threw in the fact that I'd shaken hands with Mick Foley, a popular wrestling star of the day—but I'm not sure I persuaded a single soul to become a librarian. (Then again, most librarians seem to find their way to the profession after another career has lost its luster, so perhaps the seed I planted years ago will eventually bear fruit!) Regardless, since I thoroughly enjoy my work, I had fun sharing information with students. This event gave me a great chance to connect with students and teachers away from the public library setting.

You might be amazed by the variety of programs librarians are asked to participate in. School library media specialists might be invited to come read a story during the public library's Family Reading Night or to share their views on censorship—and how it affects school library purchases—in a panel discussion at the public library during Banned Books Week. Public librarians may be asked to participate in Career Days, as I was, or may be invited to a Drop Everything and Read day at the local school. They may be called on to assist with the school's yearly book fair, either in person or by helping to promote the event. As Gail Hogan, youth services librarian, Hall County Library, Gainesville, Georgia, explains: "I try to make a note of when different schools have book fairs so that I can visit (and support their school) and let my storytime parents know where they could go for books." Accept these types of offers from other libraries; they will be very grateful.

Library card sign-ups are very popular. Many public libraries and schools work cooperatively to schedule public library visits to get students library cards. This activity might happen during a school open house, or as Mary Sheils, a school library media specialist at Stratford Middle School in Bloomingdale, Illinois, shares: "The public librarians even came during our Curriculum Night to help with signing kids up for public library cards." Both libraries see clear benefits to more students' having library cards and being able to access public library materials. This is a golden opportunity for public librarians to get more card holders (boosting those numbers again!) and to have a moment to connect with students, their parents, and staff at the schools your library serves.

If your public library does not currently have a program in place for library card sign-ups, inquire whether you can organize one yourself or whether you will need to have your circulation department assist you. Present the idea to your administration and tout the great potential of this type of program: new cardholders, increased circulation, and increased goodwill with students, parents, and the school staff. Again, this all works to build that relationship with your partner library.

Sharing Spaces

One problem many facilities face, in both the public library and the school setting, is that of limited space. Schools in expanding suburbs or crowded urban areas often must create classrooms from former teacher work areas, closets, and even lunchrooms. Computer labs take up a large amount of real estate in both schools and public libraries, and while no one feels that computers should go, the question becomes how to support existing programs under such constraints. And even if the space is available for activities, the funds may be lacking to use it properly—creating another unacceptable situation.

When considering hiring a performer or presenter for a program, first decide on the target audience and how to get it to attend. One way to increase participation is to look at the space in which a program will take place and decide how it can be used to the fullest. Here is where school library media specialists and public librarians can assist each other. If the school is not equipped to host a performer, ask whether the public library has a space that can accommodate your requirements. If the public library lacks a large meeting room, the school gym or auditorium might prove adequate. Check to see if a performance could be held (after school hours!) in a school facility.

Many types of programs can take place in shared spaces, and with programs designed for young people, it always makes sense to go to where the students are. If you are a public librarian considering starting a book discussion group for teens, why not see if the school library media specialist would like to collaborate on the project? You can work together to select the titles and come up with discussion questions. Book groups will be discussed later in this chapter but bear mentioning here in relation to decisions about space. When it comes to space concerns, allow your creativity to flow, since moving walls is usually not in anyone's yearly budget.

Feeling Brave?

Once you have accomplished a few basic cooperative projects, think about broadening your horizons and focusing on ventures that will require more time and effort from both libraries—and perhaps a greater monetary commitment. Testing the waters early on with small, safe plans helps build your confidence in each other and allows you to gauge your strengths and weaknesses as a team. Perhaps one of you is great at developing publicity materials with exciting slogans and catchy artwork, while the other enjoys communicating with others and working with performers and vendors. Use those skills and exploit them to the fullest. It is still important to keep your expectations realistic and understand what any endeavor will entail. Take a moment to consider the following before embarking on a brave new project:

- Know your goals for each project. Focusing on the desired outcome will help you decide where you need to head with the partnership and will assist you in establishing your rationale for the project.

- Think in terms of the possible benefits to your partner's library. This perspective will allow you to create a more balanced proposal before approaching another librarian.

- Realize that not every project requires a partnership. Consider your own goals and those of the other library to determine whether a partnership will benefit you both.

- Be realistic when budgeting time for the proposed project. Take out your calendar and see what other assignments are coming up. Do the eighth graders have research papers starting that week? Will you be knee-deep in databases and paper jams for a month? Are you on the planning committee for a large National Library Week program? Allow for projects' taking more than their allotted time.

- Make sure your partner's schedule is also free of major time constraints. It's never fun to feel rushed on a collaborative project because you are waiting for the other person's work.

- Give your administration a heads-up before getting in too deep. The potential project might have you out of the "office" visiting the other library, hence taking time away from your regular duties. Share your goals with your supervisor, principal, or director so they understand the basis for the collaboration and the project in general.

- Be up front and crystal clear about what you need before you begin the planning process. Money lies at the root of many disagreements, and this is true when it comes to working relationships as well. Perhaps you are considering collaboration because you want to invite a famous author to visit, but you lack either funding or space for such an event. You don't want to find out that the funds you were counting on aren't coming, but the author is.

- Make sure you each have clear expectations regarding what the other person is responsible for. Don't just assume that your counterpart is doing the publicity, for example, and find out too late that nothing has been sent to the newspapers.

Of course, many partnerships you engage in may be less structured and still work beautifully. The previous suggestions, though, are intended to cover the "just in case" situations. If you are at all concerned the partnership might not take off or might need some assistance, don't hesitate to ask questions. Create timelines so that you both have a visual understanding of your commitments. Here it is essential to have a partner with whom you can communicate easily—which is why it is sometimes best to start out with basic projects to assess each other's work styles.

Author Visits

Build your basic relationship first before scaling up to larger programs like author visits. When I first started working as a young adult librarian, I did not have much contact with the school library media specialists in the district. Once I became friendly with one of them a few years later, she happened to mention that Walter Dean Myers was coming to her school to spend the day with students. I just about fell over, green with envy. What an incredible coup to have such a famous and fabulous author speaking at the middle school! I would have killed (metaphorically, of course) to have Myers appear at our public library. My library served a very culturally diverse population, and a talk there would have resonated with a much wider audience, including parents and students from other district schools. The school that hosted Myers did not have tons of money—he visited because the school library media specialist was a friend of someone who worked at a local bookstore, which was hosting a Myers signing. The timing was wrong to get him to come to the public library as well, but I still felt like I'd lost out on a golden opportunity. Perhaps if the school

So You Want an Author?

Here are some practical considerations when embarking on a collaboration to bring in an author for a visit:

- Establish a budget, counting the funds from both libraries. If one library is fronting more money than the other, be prepared for that library to get more time with the author—technically, this is only fair. However, the author's time can be used creatively at either library.
- Find out which authors are popular with the population you are targeting. See what is being checked out at the public and school libraries, and generate a list of 10 to 20 names.
- Divide the list of names between you and your partner. Check authors' websites for available dates to see if the author does any school/public library visits and what kind of fees are involved. Make sure to find out if travel expenses are included or if there will be a separate charge.
- Revise your list, eliminating authors who are unavailable or too expensive. You may be shocked how much some authors charge, but keep in mind that many make their living this way—not everyone can be J.K. Rowling!
- Find out who's already coming to town. Check with nearby bookstores to find out about any visits they have scheduled. In this way, you might be able to get a well-known author to visit without having to foot travel expenses.
- Consider local authors, especially if funds are limited. There may be a well-known author living right in your area, if you only ask. Post the question to email lists you follow, asking for recommendations for your area. Don't forget to include information on your target population.

- Decide with your partner who will be the main contact and who will be in charge of making plans, including travel. Authors need to receive timely information on arrangements and need to know whom to call if they have questions. Plan on contacting the author by phone or email at least three or four times, adding more specifics as the date gets closer. Organization will make the event go more smoothly.
- Publicize, publicize, publicize. If no one knows about the event, no one can come. Start early, and get as much information out as possible. If a bookstore is bringing the author to town, it might be able to supply posters for you to use, and perhaps even some auto-graphed books to use as raffle or contest prizes.

library media specialist and I had ever previously chatted about the possibility of bringing in an author together, we would have been ready to seize the moment with Walter Dean Myers. This incident made me realize that, although we were close in many ways, we were not truly collaborating or even communicating with each other as well as we might for the good of our students and the community.

When people think of public library programs, author visits undoubtedly rise to the top of their list. When a PTA or PTO group gathers to discuss ways to spend their funds, the idea of an author visit usually crops up there as well. Since both groups are looking for ways to bring authors into their buildings, it seems incredible there are not more partnerships centered around author visits. Arranging a visit from a major author (basically, any writer whom more than two people recognize!) is very expensive. Often, neither the PTA/PTO nor the public library director has any idea just how high some authors' fees are. A visit from an author with any name recognition will cost anywhere from $500 (on the lowest end!) to many thousands of dollars, which may or may not include travel and hotel bills. It behooves both school and public libraries to work together and pool resources when planning an author visit.

Some communities have gotten creative and gone beyond simply bringing in a guest author. As Anne Fleming, media specialist at St. Charles North High School in St. Charles, Illinois, mentions: "For many years, the St. Charles school district library staff has enjoyed collaborating with the St. Charles Public Library. Every other year we present the St. Charles Literature Festival. The public library provides storytellers in our 17 schools while we raise funds for authors and special events. The public library staff works with us on publicity, logistical support and hosts an author-signing event. The quality of the event would not be what it is without their enthusiastic support." This type of project allows each library to have a distinct function as well as a purpose in the final literary event, and the whole community benefits from the joint efforts.

Before any author visit, you need to get students reading that author's work. If your guest has published just one book, have the students read that book. Hold a discussion group on it. If the author has written multiple books, either the school library media specialist or the public librarian (or both!) can booktalk these. The more students who have read the books, the more interest there will be in what the author has to say—whether at an assembly, at the public library, or during classroom presentations. Making sure your audience is informed and interested is all part of the publicity for the author visit and should not be discounted.

During any author visit, be sure to provide an opportunity for students and parents to buy the author's books and get them autographed. This is very important to authors as it allows them an opportunity to sell their books. Perhaps, after spending a day at the school, the author can visit the public library for a signing. Maybe the winners of a raffle could have a chance to chat personally with the author during lunch. Be creative, and enjoy spending time in the company of others who love literature as much as you do.

kids to literature, in terms of materials circulation as well as increasing readership in general.

- Three-on-three basketball – Use a sports tournament program like this to raise money for a special purpose such as an author visit or to create a special collection of library materials, such as graphic novels or new storytime books. This program has community appeal and can be repeated each year or every other year, depending on your needs and the time available.
- Film festival – Invite students to create original films for a premiere community showing at the public library. Set criteria for students to follow and allow them to write scripts and cast, film, and edit their movies. This type of project may align with state standards for student learning in technology and information literacy skills. Teachers could work with the school library media specialist to create a lesson plan for the project.

that highlight that talent. School library media specialists have a chance to enrich the lives of the students in so many positive and direct ways.

We hear a lot about bullying and its negative effect on students and on the whole school culture. As professionals, we are aware of the need for students to feel safe and that they belong to some group. This of course becomes even more important as they move from childhood into adolescence. Middle and high school students who are adrift or in a group deemed "unpopular" by their peers face real pain and can be susceptible to depression. Librarians are in a position to help these youth accept themselves and others. Think about creating a group centered around anime, manga, graphic novels, or drawing. Hold a computer gaming tournament every few months. Read *Misfits* by James Howe and *Geography Club* by Brent Hartinger to get your creative juices flowing. (Both these novels look at students on the fringe of school life who are looking for ways to survive.) Take a moment to consider possible programs on which you can partner with the other library to brighten up children's lives.

Many students enjoy the thrill of competition, either on a team or as individuals. Even students who may not be typically competitive can be surprisingly engaged when demonstrating something they truly have an interest in. Use this competitive spirit to create exciting, appealing, and worthwhile programs, and both libraries will reap the benefits. "Battles" and "tournaments" are both fun and popular, whether a Battle of the Bands or a Battle of the Books. Working with another library on these endeavors increases your odds of success, gives you access to resources you would not have on your own, and brings your community closer to the services you can provide for them. When students see a real effort being put out for them, they feel that someone truly cares about them—a feeling that is important for them to have in their lives, regardless of who provides it.

Serving Special Populations

Many libraries have formed wonderful partnerships and are taking action to create new programs for specific underserved populations in their communities. Gail Hogan, youth services librarian, Hall County Library, Gainesville, Georgia, has been working with the schools in her district. "This year I have been contacted to work in a partnership with an at-risk kindergarten. The teacher, media specialist, and I are going to come up with a plan that hopefully will help. I will be visiting once a month starting next week and taking a book (this time) to read and then we will see what we do next month." She continues by saying that "my goal this year is to visit every school's media specialist in the city and county, along with private schools and daycares, to promote the library. Should keep me busy." Because of Hogan's contact with the schools, at-risk kindergarteners benefit. This makes her effort worthwhile.

Some special populations may be served more appropriately by ongoing contact between libraries. One school library media specialist in Virginia, who works in a K–12 school for students who are deaf or blind, has set up a Shared Services Agreement with the public library in her area. This agreement provides the opportunity for her to consult with the public library's children's librarian, who assists in weeding fiction titles and developing criteria for weeding. She can also use the public library's numerous (and expensive) selection resources to help enhance the school's collection of materials.

In return, her school gives the public library information on the types of programs that might be useful and interesting for their students and provides a sign language interpreter for many events. The school also provides space for many public library programs, and plans are underway for presenting joint programs in the future. "Best of all—the public library shares their audio book collection with us. Our blind students LOVE audio books, and I don't have the funding to purchase as many as we need. The public library has a large collection, but says they don't circulate very well. So, we divide their collection into thirds. One third is housed in my library for 3 months, and then is exchanged for the next third for 3 months, etc. I keep circulation stats for the public library, which they can then include in their reports. It increases their circulation, which they like, and it gives our kids lots more choices but saves me money—a win-win for both of us!" Formal agreements, with goals and benefits stated on paper, can lend credibility to a partnership. These also help ensure stable and long-lasting arrangements, even if one member of the partnership leaves a position.

Going outside our comfort zones can be difficult but worthwhile. What populations in your school system are currently underserved? Many school districts have a school system within a system for students with severe emotional and behavioral problems. Does a school library media specialist serve these students? Does she have her own library? Is this an area in which you might work cooperatively to provide programming and materials for students who desperately need them? One high school library media specialist from Papillion, Nebraska, did just this when she teamed up with her public library. "Three years ago, the teen librarian at the public library and I began to booktalk together to the alternative high school in our area. We go about every 6 weeks. Last year, we were awarded an Oprah Winfrey grant to do a book club with teens with challenges. We did the book club with the alternative students and had a great experience." You could also consider collaborating on a teen pregnancy program. Public librarians can work with school library media specialists to establish a collection of parenting and board books, bring in storytellers, and share how the public library can be a vital resource for young parents. These types of programs work to strengthen the fabric of the society and ensure a safety net for students who may be struggling. We must work together to ensure the needs of *all* our youth are being served.

Endnote

1. Gail Bush, "Walking the Road Between Libraries: Best Practices in School and Public Library Cooperative Activities," *School Library Media Activities Monthly* 22:6 (2006): 25.

Chapter 3

Changing Seasons

Ironically, the bulk of the preparation for a public library's summer reading program occurs while temperatures hover closer to 30 degrees than 80. Public librarians are asked to begin creating their summer programs as early as fall, but most often in winter. Believe me, it can be difficult to think about warm weather while snow is blowing by the window. School library media specialists may be confused to receive a call from their public library counterpart in the middle of winter asking about free days in May or June to promote summer reading. After all, the school year isn't even half over—and likely seems to have no end in sight!

Summer reading, though, is a perfect partnership for public and school libraries. School library media specialists want to see their efforts continued over the summer, to see students reading for pleasure, for information, and to maintain their skill levels. Public librarians want to see students in the library, fill slots in their programs, increase circulation, and get great numbers to show their directors and library boards. While it makes perfect sense for both to promote and enthusiastically endorse all the aspects of a summer reading program, finding the time and energy can be difficult.

Research supports the idea that summer reading programs help increase reading scores and enable schools to spend less time reviewing in the fall. Given what a successful summer reading program can mean for youth, it is essential for public and school libraries to work together. So, how do you begin?

Promotion—AKA, Help!

At first glance, promoting summer reading programs may seem to be a concern only for public librarians. However, without assistance from the library media specialist(s) in local schools, these promotions can fall flat. At the school, students are a captive audience—while the public library can but hope they attend. Public librarians have to go where the students are to make sure young people are aware of the summer opportunities available to them. Here are some easy ways school librarians can aid public librarians in promoting summer reading programs:

- Talk to your principal about the possibility of large year-end assemblies (by grade, if possible) to introduce summer reading programs to students.

- Ask teachers if they would like to have in-class presentations on summer reading activities.

- Evaluate your year-end schedule. If you shut down the school library for inventory, and need something to occupy students during the weeks they cannot check out books, a summer reading presentation by a public librarian might be just the ticket.

- Call your local public library's children's department in the winter or early spring and set aside dates for summer reading promotion in May or June.

- Ask for posters, flyers, or newsletters advertising summer reading to post in the school library.

When you reach out to public librarians, you show them that you are invested in the success of their summer reading program. Better yet, your proactive efforts allow them access to the one place where summer reading promotion fares best: the school. These promotional efforts will depend on both libraries' situations and can range from a large assembly at the end of the year to presentations in each teacher's classroom. If the youth services department at the public library has only one full-time librarian, she is unlikely to be able to spend several days at the school encouraging summer reading attendance. On the school end, your principal may nix the idea of a large assembly, and teachers may have their classroom time planned to the last minute. In this case, the best solution may be for you to distribute a newsletter or flyer prepared by the public library and share any other information it provides. In general, though, most public library children's and young adult departments are overjoyed to be approached by a school library media specialist who wants to support their summer reading program and will move heaven and earth to send someone out to your school.

When a public librarian visits, be kind. Remember that while public librarians do work with children and teens, it is usually on a one-on-one basis. Large groups of students may be disconcerting to them. If you sense hesitation from the public librarian when you enthusiastically tell her that your principal has agreed to let her speak to three assemblies of 400-plus students, consider that she might find this somewhat intimidating. Always have a plan B. While public librarians are eager to publicize their summer reading programs, leaving the comfort of the public library and venturing into the unknown of the schools can be overwhelming for some (though for others it can be a welcome diversion!).

When public librarians approach their targeted schools, they need to be honest with themselves and their partners about where they fall along the fear-of-public-speaking continuum. No one wants to see a librarian tremble as he talks about summer reading prizes. After all, you are aiming to make kids want to come to the library, not scare them away. If you have a distinct fear of speaking in front of large groups, now is not the time to work on it. Remember, though, you are talking to *kids*, some of whom you might have known for years. (And the rest are getting out of class for an assembly, so they are disposed to like you for that reason alone!)

When thinking about promoting your public library's summer reading program to schools, be realistic about how much time you can devote. You might be surprised by how many positive responses you get, and every school may want you to come at the same time. Be clear about what you can offer. If a school needs someone to visit each class during its regularly scheduled time in the school library, but you are needed to cover the reference desk for your vacationing boss, ask about an alternative. Part of your summer planning will be to plot out the end of the school year for publicity purposes. Consider the following issues:

- How many schools have students who can participate in the library's summer reading program (consider boundary issues)?

- Have there been summer promotions to these schools in the past?

- What kind of promotion are you considering? Class visits, school assemblies, or alternative methods?

- How much time can you spend out of the library? Does your supervisor support the idea of your visiting the schools?

- Do the school library media specialists have any special needs at the end of the school year? Call to see when (and where) your visit could be most beneficial to them.

Know your target audience and the time limits, on both your side and the schools'. Ideally, a public librarian should schedule specific weeks for summer reading promotion no later than February or March. (Of course, if you have an ongoing under-standing with the schools, a quick check about specific dates around April should suffice.) Don't try to promote your programs too early, since students generally want to sign up for programs immediately after hearing about them. No one is happy to learn about programs that can't yet be signed up for.

When you first begin a summer reading promotion partnership, there are bound to be crossed wires. Perhaps teachers thought a public librarian would visit for an entire period, while the librarian figured that five minutes to pass out a flyer and introduce the program would suffice. Maybe the school principal will decide to run all of the school's last five tornado drills on one day—which happens to be summer reading day (this happened to me!). Roll with the punches, and make a mental note for next year. Going in with the understanding that you and your partner librarian will both be exhausted, mentally and physically, will bring you closer together. It's always good to learn to laugh together early on in the relationship.

I Have *How Much* Time?

Scheduling problems often result from communication problems. As discussed earlier, it is important to estimate how much time you have to offer—but reality always imposes its own schedule. The first year I went into the middle schools to promote summer reading, I had not yet begun my career as a booktalker, so I was nervous about facing students and teachers. I looked young enough to be mistaken for a student (which once made for an interesting moment when I asked how to sign myself out of a school). The school library media specialist was kind enough to set up a schedule of all the teachers who wanted someone to talk about summer reading in their classes, complete with classroom numbers, teacher names, and the approximate number of students in each (which was a lot of work on her part, since there were 700 students). However, when I actually looked at the schedule, I realized she had given me five minutes in each class—and no time to get from room to room. The rest of that day was spent in a flurry of papers shoved at students and constant apologies for being late.

This type of mistake comes out of only the best intentions. The school library media specialist was used to seeing students *in her library*. This schedule would have worked for her, but she forgot to factor in the time it took to get around the school. We laughed about this in the years after, since five minutes wasn't even enough time to introduce myself and get comfortable with the students and teachers. Still, I learned my lesson and requested more time in the future. (It also helped that in later years I already knew the teachers and where their classrooms were located!)

How much time to schedule for each class depends on several factors. Public librarians need to know how much they have to talk about. Usually, you will need to share information about both summer activities and programs and the actual reading program itself, including criteria and prizes. Typically, it is difficult to promote to more than two classes in 45 minutes. (Factor in travel time!) If the classes are coming to the school library for your presentation, you still have to be aware of how long it takes for students to leave their room, come to the library, get situated, hear the presentation, and then leave. Seeing kids in the library sounds like a great plan—until you see how long it takes to seat and quiet down 30 rambunctious fifth graders. Grouping classes together can also work, as long as teachers are vigilant about classroom management.

As the school library media specialist, you can lay the groundwork for a successful visit before the public librarian arrives. Contact the public librarian in advance to let her know what equipment she needs to bring and what the school can provide. On the day of the visit, greet her at the administration office and help with setting up any necessary props and distributing flyers. This removes some stress from your counterpart's shoulders, helping her ease into the presentation.

For visits to individual classrooms, consider doing the following to assist your public librarian:

- Compile a list of teachers who are interested in having someone explain the summer reading program.

- Create a schedule, taking into account the time it takes to travel from room to room, the bell schedule, bathroom breaks, and a joint lunch period—so the two of you can chat.

- Try to group the same ages/grades around the same times.

- If your school is large or unfamiliar to your visitor, provide a map with participating teachers' rooms clearly marked.

An assembly requires certain additional preliminary steps: The administration must approve the idea, and all teachers must be informed.

If you have time, accompany the public librarian to one or more classes to get a feel for what students may be doing over summer break. Working together to promote the program also helps give it more credibility, especially if the public librarian is relatively unknown to the students. You might offer to pass out flyers, book-talk the books offered as prizes, describe programs, and mention any incentives for joining the public library's summer reading program. Scheduling these promotional visits can be a fun part of the end of the school year, since it gives you a chance to get together with your library partner and share ideas about the students you both serve.

What Should I Do? Say? Bring?

Any interaction off your home turf can be difficult and surprising. Public librarians who have not visited a school recently need to be aware that many schools have instituted additional security measures. These range from requiring visitors to sign in at the front office to requiring them to have a personal escort the whole time they are in the building. You may be presented with a visitor's badge or nametag to wear. Just assume that these measures are for your safety, as well as that of the students. If you are scheduled in the morning, try to arrive early so that you are not caught in the chaos that always ensues right before the first bell. If you are scheduled to come later in the day, you may need to get buzzed into the school. Be sure you know the name of the school library media specialist or at least one teacher you are visiting that day. Check with the school library media specialist for any important instructions about where and how to enter the school. Will you need a photo ID? What do you do after you have checked in at the main office?

So, what should a public librarian bring along on a school visit for summer reading promotion? Start with the following ideas, and consult your school library media specialist for specifics:

- Money for lunch, but also a snack (in case you can't get into the cafeteria)

- Bottled water and cough drops—you'll be doing lots of talking

- All your summer reading promotion paraphernalia and your photo ID (but try not to bring a purse or other personal items, as there may be no place to store them safely while presenting)

- A copy of your schedule and a map of the school

- Summer reading club flyers that include a program calendar and/or a newsletter describing the library's summer activities

- Instructions on how to sign up for and participate in the reading program

- Pictures or examples of the projects kids will be making in any summer craft programs you have scheduled

Paper is heavy, so if you have hundreds of students to visit in one day, see if you can leave handouts in the school library and replenish your supply as needed. When presenting, always allow some time for questions.

Most public librarians aren't proficient in classroom management. (This will be discussed in more detail in Chapter 8.) Be aware of the need to manage students, even when you are only in front of the class for 15 or 20 minutes. After all, it's the end of the school year, and everyone is jumpy and itching to be done with school. Here is where the assistance of the school library media specialist can be invaluable. Have a candid discussion with her about basic classroom etiquette and procedures before proceeding with summer reading promotion. School library media specialists should inform the public librarian in advance if certain classes may be particularly difficult, and perhaps even come along to those classes to help ensure a positive experience. This also gives you another chance to develop your professional relationship.

The type of summer reading presentation you give depends on your personal style. I tend to joke my way through booktalks and summer reading presentations and try not to take myself too seriously. A lighthearted approach can be hard, since you have no doubt spent hours working on summer activities. Remember, though, you are working with kids—who are just thinking about not having homework for the next few months. If a class seems unresponsive and uninterested, don't take it personally. You might be shocked to see their smiling faces in a few weeks, asking about that "Pluck a Duck" program you described. Keep your head high, smile, and be sure to find the school library media specialist and thank her for setting everything up. (You might also ask how she manages to do her job every day and keep her sanity intact!)

Alternatives to Face-to-Face Contact

So, all the excitement of the end of the school year is upon you. You are a school library media specialist, you contact the public library to ask about summer reading promotion, and you are told that the library doesn't have the time or staff to send someone to your school. Does this mean an end to your hopes for student reading this summer? Even with the best of intentions, we have all seen how time can get away from us—and this can certainly happen easily during the rush to put together a summer reading program. Or perhaps the public library is simply too small to spare the staff for an in-school presentation. Here are some alternative ways to promote the summer reading program, which will benefit both the school and the public library.

Newsletters or Flyers

Newsletters or flyers are a vital part of publicizing summer activities, and many public libraries produce these for summer reading participants. Schools can ask whether such a handout exists and request copies for students. If the public library has only a limited number of newsletters, perhaps the school could print additional copies or have copies on hand in the school library for interested students. Flyers or posters about individual programs can also be posted in the school library; this is another good way to grab students' attention and let them know what will be happening locally during the summer.

School library media specialists can also promote summer reading by doing presentations for their students on behalf of the public library. Get information about the program from the public librarian, as well as any props (such as sample craft projects) and flyers or newsletters to distribute. Does your school library remain open during the summer? If so, ask if the public library would like to extend its program to your building. Why duplicate its efforts? Just be sure to keep track of the numbers so that the public library can count your students as participants.

Summer Reading DVDs

Public librarians can promote summer reading by producing a DVD with pertinent information and distributing copies to the schools. A DVD can be fun to create and a great choice when there are a large number of schools in the public library district to cover. On your DVD, highlight summer programs, activities, and the reading program itself. This is the perfect opportunity to involve other public library staff members and teen advisory group members, and you can also establish new links to the schools as you distribute the DVD via the school librarians. You can post the video on the public library's website as well and inform the schools of its presence to help focus attention on your program.

If you decide to make a promotional DVD for your summer reading program, you'll have to determine how elaborate you want this project to be. One year, rather than doing in-person summer reading promotion, I worked with several teens and two other staff members to create a video to distribute in the schools. Our summer reading participation levels dropped that year, so the following year I returned to the exhausting job of promoting to each school in person. Nevertheless, if you are pressed for time or serve a large number of schools, you should consider a DVD as an alternative to no promotion at all. It can also make a great addition to face-to-face contact.

Start by evaluating your hardware and software, making sure that at least one computer in your building has a DVD burner. If you want to include video on your DVD, you will need a camcorder, as well as video editing software to put it together. If you don't have access to a camcorder, don't worry—video is not a must. Enlist the help of students—they might be used to making movies and would love to help the librarian. Do you have a scanner or a digital camera? Use these to create graphics and photos to give your promotional piece more excitement.

Software that might be useful in DVD creation includes:

- Adobe Premiere Elements (PC) – This consumer-grade movie-making software lets you edit video and export it to DVD.

- iDVD (Mac) – Export Keynote or iMovie files to iDVD to burn DVDs for the schools.

- iMovie (Mac) – Easy-to-use consumer video editing software included on newer Macs.

- Keynote (Mac) – Keynote, included in iWorks, functions similarly to PowerPoint and allows you to use video, images, and voice-over to create a looping presentation that runs by itself.

- PowerPoint (Mac or PC) – While many people are familiar with PowerPoint as presentation software, it also allows

you to create an unattended presentation that runs
(and repeats) automatically.

- Publisher (Mac or PC) – Use Publisher to create flyers,
  which you can then import as an image into Movie Maker
  or other video software.

- Windows Movie Maker (PC) – This software lends itself
  very well to a DVD project, allowing you to include music,
  video, still digital pictures, and titles.

Once you have completed your movie, you will want to burn
copies for the schools using the DVD burning software on your
computer. There are many different packages to choose from; one
is likely included on your machine if it has a DVD burner.

When making this DVD, have fun! Add your own personal flair,
and don't hesitate to involve as many children and/or teens as possible. Hold auditions for your movie, shoot video of kids making
the crafts you plan for summer, have students do the voice-over
describing the reading program, and include testimonials from
students who participated in the summer program the year before.
Try including the following in your movie:

- The name and location of your library

- The start and end dates for your summer reading program

- A list of programs, including craft programs and special
  performers, computer classes, and storytimes

- Photos of sample crafts and any guest presenters—with
  video if possible

- Rules for the summer reading program

- The prizes for participating (with pictures)

- Pictures of the library, including outside shots, circulation
  desks, the children's area, the young adult area, and other
  spots participants might need to know about

- Fun introductions to the library staff members whom children will be encountering during the summer

- Library hours of operation during the summer—especially if they are different from the hours during the school year

- Web address of the library

- Pictures of students participating in previous years' summer activities

As always, include whatever makes the most sense for the group you are targeting. If you are creating a quick five-minute reminder DVD for K–3 students, focus on activities they will like, but leave out the details. For young adults, focus on the prizes and highlight programs you think they will enjoy by giving them more information. Consider putting your movie on a television or PC at the library to run all summer long. Upload it to your website, blog, MySpace page, and YouTube account (see Chapter 6 for more on using technology). Get creative and try to include as many staff and students as possible in the production to give it a broader appeal.

With relatively modest resources, careful planning, and adequate time, you have many avenues for promoting summer reading. After all, it is in the best interests of the youth both libraries serve to keep them reading over the summer break. The possibilities for working together are endless.

Where to Find Summer Reading Lists

I saw a sign in my local bookstore the other day saying that it had copies of all the local school summer reading lists. This is, of course, a brilliant strategy on the store's part since chances are that parents will then buy these books there. It's funny how libraries seem to be playing catch-up with the bookstores these days. We hear a lot in the library community about how to market our services and materials, and here is a prime example. It makes perfect sense for every public library to have the summer reading lists for local schools and to make sure they have the required titles in their collection. Many do, but this is not always the case.

Maintaining a file of summer reading lists is a very simple way for librarians to work together to help alleviate parent and student frustration during the summer—when, of course, the child has lost the summer reading list he received at the end of the school year, since homework was the last thing on his mind. Cooperation here helps establish a relationship between the two libraries, as well. Just as with the summer reading program, both parties have a stake in having the lists and materials on hand.

School library media specialists should try to get summer reading lists to their public librarian by the beginning of April, so the library can order additional copies of the books if necessary (or at least make sure they have all the titles). Ensure that each list clearly states what level it is intended for (such as all sixth graders, or tenth graders taking Honors English), and make sure the school's name is prominently displayed. Some schools now post their summer reading lists on their websites. If your school does this, let the public library know so that it can add a link to its website or print out the information.

While things are revving up for summer reading, public librarians need to remember to ask each school about summer reading lists and stock copies; these lists will be important for readers' advisory during the summer chaos. School library media specialists will be working hard to get things in order before school closes for the summer, so don't count on them to provide the lists. Find out if the titles on these lists are suggested or required reading, as this will help you determine collection needs. Share the information with other staff members, especially circulation and reference staff. Keep in mind that students will ask any person they see working at the library for these lists, so having them clearly marked and easily found will aid everyone.

Once again, this project may seem simple, but it does take some effort. The payoff, though, can be great for both libraries. Working together on small projects like reading lists helps create links, and once you have contacted each other to ask for small favors, it is easier to move on to larger collaborative endeavors.

Gearing Up for Fall

As public librarians are recovering from their intense summer reading programs, school library media specialists are gearing up for the coming school year. They are working on lesson plans, compiling lists of titles to purchase, and touching base with teachers. Though this might not seem like a good time to partner on projects, it truly is. School librarians are refreshed from their summer break and, if not eager, then at least optimistic about starting a new school year. Public librarians have hopefully had a few weeks to relax after the end of summer reading. Now is the perfect time to propose some small cooperative efforts to pave the way into another productive year.

Volunteers ... in the Library?

Public librarians often receive calls from teachers inquiring whether the public library is open to having volunteers from the National Honor Society (or its younger cousin, National Junior Honor Society). Students may need to meet service requirements, and the public library can help by employing student volunteers. Links established between the school and public library at the beginning of the school year can be valuable later when a teacher is scrambling to find volunteer opportunities. School library media specialists can check with the public library to find out if it lets students earn volunteer credit toward service hours. Public librarians can think in terms of all the help student volunteers could offer. You can have them:

- Shelfread

- Shelve books

- Assist with storytimes

- Help out with young adult programs

- Help cut out and assemble craft materials for storytimes or other children's programs

- Assist with summer reading activities

- Provide computer help or teach computer classes to younger kids or seniors

The possibilities are limited only by your director and library board; there are many options for using student volunteers in the public library. Working to establish this connection with the schools will aid both the school library media specialist (who can tell the group sponsor where students can get service hours) and the public librarian (who gets free labor); it also helps strengthen the bond between the school and public library.

State Reading Contests: To Buy or Not to Buy?

In Illinois, the winner of Rebecca Caudill Young Reader's Book Award is decided by school children, who select their favorite book from a list of 20 titles. Each year, schools across Illinois encourage students to read titles from the list of nominees and vote for the one that appeals to them. Promotion of the award process begins in the fall and continues until the votes are tallied and the winner announced at a literary conference in March. Since the Caudill Award targets students in fourth through eighth grade, Illinois has created two other awards focusing on younger and older students. Many other states hold similar award contests, in which students get to choose the book that speaks to them. (A comprehensive list can be found at www.carr.org/read/stateawardbks.htm.) Each award has its own criteria, but typically these programs are set up to run within the school year. And while they usually fall under the purview of the schools, many public libraries also hold their own contests.

Book awards provide a fantastic opportunity for school and public libraries to work together to promote reading. School libraries may need to obtain multiple copies of the nominated titles, which change from year to year. While it is great to give students access to all these titles and enable participation in the voting process, supplying the books can be a budget killer for many schools, and some of them in fact may not be able to participate due to a lack of funds. Working in partnership with the local public library provides a perfect solution to this dilemma.

Public librarians are always concerned with the circulation statistics of their collections. The higher the usage, the happier they are. Book contests are a perfect way for public libraries to increase statistics while at the same time giving students access to materials for pleasure reading. Kids think it is great when a book they have read and voted for wins a competition. Public librarians can talk with the school library media specialist to see if the school currently participates in any state reading contests. (Be prepared to provide an example of one in your state, in case the school wants more information.) School library media specialists can approach public librarians with the list of titles nominated for the current year. Explain that having multiple copies of these books on hand would benefit both libraries, since you will be promoting these titles and do not have a sufficient supply. Once this conversation is initiated, you might invite the public librarian in to do a booktalk on these titles or create a joint Battle of the Books program based on the nominees, to be held at the public library.

Going with the Flow

Summer can be a great time for reading, fun, and beginning a relationship with a partner library. Fall brings back-to-school energy that can provide a springboard for collaboration throughout the year. Spend time, energy, and money in the places with the biggest potential return, and work with your colleague to determine the best avenues for your joint resources. Don't let summer end without reaching out to your counterpart in the other building, and begin the fall on the right collaborative foot and with the spirit of partnership already growing.

Chapter 4

After-School Blues

Recent studies have challenged the notion that the night hours are the most perilous to unsupervised children. They point out that the hours between the end of the school day and the time that parents or other primary caregivers come home can spell the most trouble for school-age "children in self-care," in terms of where they are and what they are doing.

—Rebecca Singer[1]

Eight years of working in a public library gave me plenty of time to think about the youth who come to the library after school. One library in my district was located next to a high school, and our daily influx of teens was incredible. Our second library was literally on the other side of the parking lot of an elementary school. Trust me, we never needed to look at the clock to know exactly what time school was out; we simply looked out over the vast expanse of students' faces. Despite the presence of a security guard, this situation became overwhelming, with mobs of teens roaming the library at will and leaving destruction in their wake. This was especially frustrating to me as the YA librarian—I was supposed to be the advocate for these students, yet at the same time, I had to play enforcer. Things finally came to a head, and we invited the local police officers who were stationed at the high school to come in and assist our weary security guard. Our director also realized that two floors of a building was simply too much territory for one person to cover during the after-school rush, so we later hired another security guard.

Through trial and error, our library eventually learned to manage the daily deluge of students coming in to do homework, socialize, use the computers, socialize, find reading materials—and socialize! You get the picture. This type of situation often puts the librarians who work closely with youth under pressure from other staff members to control the chaos. After all, we do want to assist these young people, encourage them to come to the library, and help them see it as a safe and inviting space to interact with their peers and with adults. However, not all library staff members may see kids in the same light.

School library media specialists may wonder what this chapter even has to do with them. You already deal with behavior issues at your own institution and don't need to "borrow trouble," as it were. Since public and school libraries are linked on so many levels, though, it is imperative for both to address the after-school issue. Nothing beats down a relationship faster than resentment, which is what situations like this can lead to. Some public library administrators believe that schools receive the lion's share of the pot in terms of funding (although many school library media centers are actually woefully underfunded). If the public library has difficulty with students after school, it may even be inclined to cut back services to the schools—however irrational that may be. Meaningful partnerships are difficult, if not impossible, if the public library administration is bogged down in dealing with upset staff and community members. So, while at first glance this might seem like a public library issue, it really becomes a community issue, and one in which the school librarians, who know and work with these kids, can be a big help. Since the school and public libraries are allied, it makes sense for this to be a common battle—where both sides win.

Not a Babysitter!

A common complaint among both educators and public library staff members is that parents turn their children over to schools or leave them at public libraries and expect staff members just to deal with them. Both teachers and public library staff struggle with how best to handle the youth in their institutions. A major reason teachers leave the profession within the first five years is having to deal with classroom management issues. School library media specialists must deal with these issues as well, since many can count on being the sole adult in the school library during class visits. In fact, the school library is often the place where elementary teachers leave their students during their planning period. As more principals become aware of the benefits of a flexible schedule, though, this is changing, and some schools give school library media specialists time to collaborate with teachers and public librarians.

Most teachers and school library media specialists have had some formal training in classroom management—although it never seems to be enough. Public librarians, on the other hand, have had none. There are no library school courses that instruct public librarians in the do's and don'ts of dealing with unruly children. How to deal with a challenge to a book? Yes. How to stop teenagers from doing cartwheels down the aisles? No. While public librarians may bemoan the fact that children are turned loose unattended in the library, this is nevertheless a fact that must be dealt with—just as teachers and school administrations must figure out policies to ensure the safety of students while providing a nurturing learning environment. So how can we work together to ensure that libraries are enjoyable for *all* who enter?

Start this dialogue just as you would any other. Of course, one side must initiate the conversation—but once that happens, things will take off quickly. School librarians can check to see if the public library is experiencing trouble with students and if there are particular problem areas or times. While the public librarian may be leery of sharing this information with you, he may just as well be desperate for an understanding ear. Remember, schools deal with discipline issues on a daily basis. They are usually much better equipped with positive methods for alleviating problems. On the other hand, public libraries do have the option of demanding that the offending person leave the premises. This seems to be a favorite solution but doesn't really solve the problem, as there is always another one waiting in the wings. The following are some ways school library media specialists can help both their beleaguered public library colleagues and themselves:

- Check in a few times during the school year to see if there is a problem brewing. When kids are antsy at school, they are likely to be antsy at the public library. Sometimes just sharing the fact that students are going crazy at the school as well is enough to help.

- Get a group of seasoned teachers to provide feedback on what works for them in the classroom setting in gaining the attention and respect of their students. Share these ideas with the public librarians so that they have something more than instinct to guide them.

- Arrange for public librarians to visit the classrooms of some of these experienced teachers to observe how they interact with the students.

- Arrange for a group of teachers to meet after school at the library to share information with the public library staff.

- If your school has a system in place to reward desired behavior, invite the public library to share in this system. For example, some schools use fake money that students can accumulate for good behavior and use to "purchase" things from a school store. Give the public library staff a supply of this "money" so they can hand it out to students they see acting in an appropriate manner.

- Work with your library partner to create library-related incentives for positive behavior. For instance, if a student brings four books back on time to the school library consecutively, he might get a special "fine forgiveness" card that can be used at the public library or school library. Public libraries could also use these fine forgiveness cards to reward good behavior. Establish parameters for your reward system, and track incidents of bad behavior and expulsions from the public library over time to gauge the effectiveness of the program.

- Arrange for a public librarian to come to the school and speak to students (in a humorous way is always best!) about some of the issues involving students at the public library. Once, when things were really bad, I spent some of my booktalk time at the school discussing various activities we were seeing in the library at the time—playing hockey with the books, dancing on the tables, hide-and-seek in the stacks—and writing these on the board. The students thought some of the things were hilarious, but they all recognized that these were not behaviors we tolerated in the public library. Just having someone talk about the situation gave us more control, showing students that we were watching and that we were taking steps to stop these activities.

Let students know that your libraries are working together to make sure everyone has a pleasant experience in both libraries. This reinforces the belief that libraries are an important and valuable resource in the community.

Some public libraries are fortunate to have security guards on location after school, but their effectiveness is largely dependent on their personality. If your library's security monitor is very intent on getting teens to admit their wrongdoing or tends to "stalk" kids while they are in the library, this overzealousness may simply cause new problems. Public librarians can work with their administration to stress that driving away people who want to use the library (even if simply to socialize after school) is detrimental to the vitality of the library as a social institution. This might allow you to find a more productive security monitor or modify your current one's approach. Offer to have him meet with some teachers to see how they handle both group situations and one-on-one interactions. Also, be sure to tap your local police force for any information they may have about working with kids. Check with the school system to see if it has officers who are assigned to work in the school or with the student population as part of their regular duties.

The reality of working in a public library is that you will see latchkey kids—lots of them. Knowing how to interact with them is important; take the time to develop a base of resources to draw on when times become difficult. Realize that the school staff works with students every day and has the background needed to deal with certain situations, as well as experience that most public library staff lack. There is no crime in asking for help.

One way to channel the energy of children and teens who have nothing better to do than play tag in the library is to give them library programs to attend once a week. Creating a true after-school program might be outside your scope, but providing fun, interactive adventures for kids in a monitored setting can help curb some undesirable behavior. Find ideas in Chapters 2 and 6 for book discussions, gaming programs, podcasts, YouTube videos, and summer reading projects. Programs such as these just might give children the creative outlet they seek and provide the public library some great program attendance statistics. Along the way, don't be surprised if you develop lasting relationships—of the good variety—with your former troublemakers.

Homework, Anyone?

Homework help centers have grown tremendously popular over the years as public libraries recognize the value of providing materials and assistance for children and teens geared specifically toward schoolwork. These centers vary from library to library, with some simply having a few reference books allocated for homework and others having dedicated space that includes computers, textbooks, reference materials, tutors, and databases. "Reasons for providing homework help are either internally driven, such as the library's need to control a critical latchkey situation, or motivated by external forces, such as fulfilling a citywide mandate to offer after-school prevention programs for at-risk youth. At the very least, a library's homework help program offers kids a designated place to go after school where they can get help with their class work. At its best, the program offers positive human interaction and scholastic support that might otherwise be missing from the youngster's life."[2] Work with the school system(s) in your area to help create a relevant and useful center for students and teachers. This is another area in which the public librarian and the school library media specialist can cooperate to achieve similar goals in their different locations.

If your public library already offers a homework help center, check to see how often the materials are used and whether they match the present curriculum. Curricula often change every few years, and a homework center can easily become outdated if no one checks to make sure the resources are current. One key ingredient for a successful homework center is to have all the schools' textbooks available. Students often forget their textbooks at school, or they remember an assignment is due at the last minute and need to access a textbook immediately. (There is a reason Sunday tends to be a very busy day at many public libraries!) Be sure to check the textbooks a few times a year, because they often "disappear." Sometimes school districts will supply the public library with textbooks; other times the public library will need to purchase these materials itself. Think of these purchases as adding a valuable resource to your collection, just as when buying other reference books.

Online databases have become increasingly important for student work. As a public librarian, take some time to see how your databases link with the curriculum and mention these connections to the school library media specialist. For instance, if high school students must do critical analyses of literary works, see if the public library has literature-related databases to meet that need. Likewise, as a school library media specialist, you can check to see if the public library's current databases would benefit your students or give suggestions for future purchases, emphasizing how a particular database will be used by students. Since their resources are limited, public libraries are always more willing to invest funds in a product that they know will definitely serve some portion of their population. (Find more information on resource sharing, including databases, in Chapter 7.)

Public libraries should see what is already available in the community before launching a large homework help center. Many schools now offer an after-school program with homework help, snacks, and exercise. More and more parents work during the day, and once students become too old for traditional daycare, schools step in to fill the gap. Unfortunately, many of school programs cover only the elementary levels, leaving middle and high school students at a disadvantage. If this is the situation in your community, perhaps the public library can devote more funding and resources to a homework help center for the middle and upper grade levels.

In conjunction with homework centers, tutors can be invaluable sources of assistance—though they can also be a burden if the program does not take off or becomes stagnant. At my former workplace, a retired teacher looking for some way to fill a few afternoons a week volunteered to assist students with their math homework. This idea sounded great, but we rarely had students who wanted to work with him. There may have been an intimidation factor at work, since this man was older and the students had never had him as a teacher. Another factor was that we did not actually have a space set aside for homework help, so students were not expecting a tutor to be there to help them. If you decide to use tutors to enhance the public library homework help center, here are some things to consider:

- School library media specialists should check to see if any teachers are interested in assisting students one night a week at the public library. Look for funding, either through a grant or within the education system, so that you are able to offer teachers some kind of stipend. Public librarians can ask their administration about paying teachers a small fee from library funds, or they can look into grants for this purpose.

- Solicit older students as volunteer peer tutors. Some schools require National Honor Society students to perform a certain number of community service hours, and some high schools require students to do community service to graduate, which creates a natural pool from which to draw these volunteers.

- Make sure there is a dedicated space for tutors. Rotating spaces can be confusing, both to students looking for help and to the tutors themselves—not to mention staff members.

- Keep the same times and days for the tutoring throughout the entire school year. Don't discourage a child who has finally worked up the courage to ask for help, only to find it isn't available when it was advertised.

- Establish someone to schedule the tutors and designate a backup for when that person is unavailable. (Questions about the service—where it is located, who the tutors are, and who can use the service—always come up after the person in charge has left for the day!) Having someone else "in the know" helps alleviate confusion. Library staff need to know whom to go to with questions from the public, and the tutors need someone to contact as well.

- Create a brochure answering frequently asked questions about tutoring so that library staff can hand it out to interested students and parents.

- Make sure your brochure and any other advertising specify what level of help is being offered. Let parents know if homework helpers are other students or certified teachers.

If you manage to find funds to pay teachers or other professional tutors to work in the center, chances are you will have little trouble with staffing. Volunteers may not have the same level of commitment, especially if they are simply fulfilling a time requirement for some other organization. Also keep in mind that you may lose some of your student volunteers during certain times of the year if they are involved in extracurricular activities—or if their interest level wanes.

Staffing a program with volunteers can be a hassle, so consider all your options and goals before making a lasting commitment to a tutoring help center. Create a list of criteria for continuing the program, including attendance, reliability of the tutors, and staff time required, so you can evaluate its success after a certain period of time. Give yourselves an out. List exactly how you will decide if the program has been a success—but know that some part of your evaluation will be based on anecdotal evidence such as teacher and student comments. Perhaps only three students a week make use of the program, but your tutors are faithful and dependable, and little of your time is spent in managing them. This, in your eyes, might be a success. Alternatively, you may want to see at least 50 students using the service each week in order to make the time and effort spent worth your while.

Know your goals in establishing a tutoring program and be realistic with regard to what you and your libraries can offer. As involved as a school library media specialist might want to be, the homework help center will be set up in the public library. The location, in and of itself, will limit her hands-on participation in the program. Don't be too discouraged if your tutoring program fails to take off. Do give it a chance, however, and don't pull the plug too soon. Try to maintain the program for at least one full school year so that students are given the opportunity to see it is there, and publicize it so that the program has a fair chance of success.

If the idea of scheduling tutors doesn't get you all that excited, consider using online methods to accomplish some of the same goals. Many public libraries offer access to Tutor.com, an online homework help service. Tutor.com has teachers available online during set time periods to assist fourth through twelfth grade students with their homework. Check to see if any public libraries in your area use this service, and ask whether they feel it meets their goals and needs. If the local public library offers this online resource, school library media specialists can make sure students are aware of it. If not, do some research to see if it might make sense for your community. If funding is the issue, perhaps joint monies could be used to make the service available on a trial basis.

Other online possibilities include allowing patrons to ask reference or homework questions via email or providing real-time chat (through an instant messaging service) with public reference librarians. If you are in a school, and your public library offers this type of service, check to see which department is in charge and when librarians are online. (Live reference assistance may only be offered during certain hours.) Ask if a public library representative can come and demonstrate the service to students in the school library. If you are in a public library, contact the school library media specialist and explain the service. Be clear about when the service is available, and make sure, if you publicize it, that it is adequately staffed.

Some public libraries also offer homework help by providing a list of relevant websites for students. As the school library media specialist, work with your counterpart in the public library to keep her up-to-date on new curriculum topics. Share any particularly useful websites you find so that these can be listed both on the public library's homework site and the school library's web page. The more places the information is available, the more likely students will find it; working together, libraries can create a comprehensive one-stop shop for students.

The best way to provide homework help in your community will depend on many factors, including what resources are currently in place, how they are meeting the needs of the students, the funding and time you have available, and what you can realistically hope to accomplish. Know your own and your partner's time, space, and budgetary constraints. This preparation will help you decide what the important issues are and how best to address them.

Acknowledging the Problem

Sometimes the hardest part of attacking a given problem or situation is just accepting that it exists in the first place. Many librarians go into the field dreaming of wood floors, comfortable chairs, rows of books, and lots of solitude and quiet. Of course, this is an antiquated idea, but the stereotype of the library still persists—not only in the minds of the public, but also in the minds of many who work there. Each library faces its own challenges in terms of dealing with youth, and each must establish its own criteria to manage less-than-desirable behavior. Realize how school and public libraries can assist each other in the long run, and find that middle ground where both parties are excited about the *possibilities* of students in the library, rather than the *liabilities*.

Endnotes

1. Rebecca Singer, "School-age Children and the Public Library," *Journal of Youth Services in Libraries* 13:1 (1999): 37.
2. Cindy Mediavilla, "Why Library Homework Centers Extend Society's Safety Net," *American Libraries* 32:11 (2001): 40.

Chapter 5

From Basic to Bravo!

Moving from basic to bravo with cooperative projects and partnerships requires that you expand your programs. The idea of collaboration as a community goal might be a change, and it must have the support of more than just two librarians in two libraries. For larger, grander collaborations to be successful, you need the continued backing of your administrations, funding sources, and often the support of organizations outside the library community. An awareness of the potential benefits these expansive projects can bring to a community, though, will assist in creating a shared vision among all the participants.

Beyond Brave

Your school library started working with the public library, and you realized it would be great fun to hold a joint basketball tournament to raise funds for both libraries. However, while your principal is on board, the superintendent wants to know why all the other schools aren't involved, too. What happens when parents from the other schools start asking, why can't my child participate? Suddenly, your school/public library collaboration has turned into a firestorm of controversy! How can you make the shift from working with one library to working with multiple libraries without causing major stress?

Before you move into this next phase, it is important to have a serious conversation with ... yourself. Make sure there isn't a simpler way to achieve your objective(s), without launching a communitywide—or even several-entitywide—project. While these large-scale organizational efforts are important and rewarding, they require a great deal of time and energy. Use the following checklist to see if you and your community are ready for bigger and better things:

- You and at least one other library have worked well together on a minimum of three projects.

- At least one project involved a monetary commitment from each party—and there were no complications.

- Each library involved has several people interested in collaborating, not just one individual.

- Upper management was supportive of past projects and has expressed interest in seeing what other possibilities are on the horizon.

- You are comfortable working with all potential partners.

- You have a clear idea of how much time you can invest.

Even if the entire checklist is a go, be prepared to deal with unforeseen events. What happens if a supervisor leaves and her replacement does not support the idea? What happens if money that was allocated for a project gets redistributed, or an institution's priorities change? It is impossible to prepare for every potential problem, but be realistic from the beginning.

Local Partnerships

Many large library and school districts are seeing the benefits of creating partnerships to share resources and information. Public libraries know that their mission requires them to work with the school population, both students and teachers, while school systems want to maximize student opportunities for learning. The Howard County Library in Columbia, Maryland, for example, has developed a program in conjunction with the public school system called A+ Partners in Education. According to its website:

In September 2002, Howard County Library and the Howard County Public School System began a new countywide initiative: A+ Partners in Education. Our mission is to develop programs, activities, and events for all Howard County students, their families and teachers that increase love of reading, advocate the completion of school assignments, promote scholarship, and ensure academic success. In addition, we encourage every Howard County Public School student to own and use a Howard County Library card to borrow materials and access databases. With the passage of the No Child Left Behind Act of 2001, this initiative is especially important as all schools seek to improve their students' overall reading and writing skills.[1]

The online component of A+ Partners in Education provides information for students and parents, including an online zine for teens and test-taking hints. For school library media specialists and teachers, there is a section that offers curriculum enhancement guides for elementary, middle, and high school. These highlight specific programs designed to coordinate with the school curriculum. Directions on how to apply for and participate in this project are clearly available, and the attention to detail is evident. The Howard County Library has taken the time to outline what has made its program a success and how the library went about creating and sustaining this partnership. It has put it all together online in the A+ Partnership Toolkit (www.hclibrary.org/index.php?page=14).

Public library partnerships with multiple schools are catching on across the country. Visitors to the website of the Dauphin County Library System (DCLS) in Harrisburg, Pennsylvania, (www.dcls.org) will notice a special page for parents and teachers. Visitors will find recommended reading lists by grade level, information on teaching and lesson planning, and a downloadable newsletter for educators, which includes information on current and forthcoming public library programs, resources for educators, and new materials of special interest.

The DCLS website also includes a PowerPoint presentation, publicized both on the site and in its quarterly newsletter, to promote its summer reading program to school library media specialists. The library maintains ongoing close ties with the school library media specialists to promote the summer program in individual schools. Since the DCLS system serves more than 100 schools, it would be impossible for any one person—or even a small army of librarians!—to see every class personally before the end of the school year. Using school library media specialists to promote the summer reading program allows DCLS to connect with students it could not otherwise reach, given limited time and personnel. This collaborative effort also gives these school librarians a stake in the public library's program and lets them work together with the public library to create stronger readers. (See Chapter 3 for more on cross-promoting summer reading programs.)

Across the country in Oregon, the Multnomah County Library (which serves approximately one-fifth of the state's population) has a program in place called School Corps. The library's goal "is to increase the information literacy of Multnomah County students by working in partnership with local schools."[2] Multnomah County employs five School Corps librarians, who provide programs and support to the school library media specialists and teachers in the county. School Corps services support the curriculum with offerings such as customized bibliographies, pathfinders, and booklists for requested grade levels.

One of the longest-running collaborative school/public library partnerships is New York's Connecting Libraries and Schools Project, more commonly known as CLASP. This program began in 1991 at the New York Public Library with a grant from the DeWitt Wallace-Reader's Digest Fund and continues to this day. "CLASP initially worked with three community school districts containing twenty-three public library branches and 107 schools. The program was so successful that the three public library systems worked together to propose to the New York city council that CLASP be expanded citywide. In 1994, CLASP was implemented in all five boroughs of New York City."[3] So, what does CLASP do, and how does it work? Its main goals are as follows: maintain an active collaborative and cooperative function between the public libraries and New York schools, stress family literacy and learning as well as enjoyment, and highlight libraries and all they provide to the community.[4] As with many such partnerships, these goals are met through booktalks, library card drives, programs, and working collaboratively with school library media specialists and teachers. This program stands out for the sheer size of the population it serves and for the success it has found in addressing the needs of such an extensive and diverse group of people. Although this program began with private funding, the first three years were so productive that a proposal to extend it was brought before the city council—which understood the importance of the program and ensured its continued existence by authorizing funding for materials and personnel.

Get It Together

When searching the literature for information about collaboration between schools and public libraries, you will often come across descriptions of school/public library combinations. These are typically called *joint use* libraries since they serve as both public and school libraries. There are many reasons to contemplate creating a joint use library, but these usually boil down to one thing: funding. Why build two libraries when you can build one and have it serve two functions?

While on the surface this seems a perfect blending, there can be some sticking points along the way that prevent these types of libraries from being more widespread. Who will fund the joint use library? Who will maintain the library? Who will staff and manage the library? And, of course, who will control the collection, materials, databases, software, hardware, etc.? As Alan Bundy and Larry Amey mention, many examples in the literature point out "the susceptibility of joint use libraries to dysfunctionality or even failures, although the record of successful combinations is improving

Connecting Big Citywide

An interview with Kate Todd, Connecting Libraries and Schools Project (CLASP), director, 1993–2000.

Q. Did you initiate any kind of contact with your local schools/school library media centers?
A. Yes. We had contact at all levels, from school library media specialists in local schools up to the director of School Library Services for New York City. There were different projects that could be undertaken at each level.

Q. What kind of a reaction did you get from these schools/school library media specialists?
A. School library media specialists were happy to have contact with other librarians since they were often the only librarian in a staff of teachers who knew little about running a library. Also, their status was increased when they brought public librarians, as resource people, to work with the schools.

Q. Did you specifically promote certain programs? For example, did you go into the schools and talk about summer reading programs?
A. We developed teachers' collections containing books and magazines about educational theories and curriculum ideas. These collections were promoted for teachers in order to bring them into library branches.

Q. Did you create any specific kinds of partnerships with the schools that you could explain here?
A. We hosted the annual school librarian staff development at local library branches. This both allowed us to learn what was important to them and let them see public library resources.

Q. How was the administration in terms of support when it came to working with the schools?

A. There is a multilevel administration within the library, and various people had different attitudes about the importance of collaboration. Some people welcomed the partnership because it provided valuable services to children, teachers, and parents. Others felt that schools get enough of the city budget and should not get more support from public librarians.

Q. Did you have any success in showing the administration how important this collaboration is?

A. There was substantial support from elected officials for the collaborative project. The addition of $6 million to the library budget for collaborative activities demonstrated its importance to library administrators.

Q. Is there anything else you would like to say about partnering with school libraries?

A. Collaboration is sometimes difficult because of the different organizational cultures in schools and libraries. This can cause misunderstandings and unrealistic expectations. The first step toward an effective partnership is learning about the other work environment.

Disclaimer: These are personal views and in no way reflect an official position of the New York Public Library.

because of informed planning and consideration of the requirements for success."[5] How each issue is resolved depends greatly on individual communities. Some joint use libraries receive the majority of their funding from the school district for construction of the building, while operating and staffing costs fall on the public library district. In some cases, a school library media specialist is on staff and controls her own collection, while the public library area has its own separate collection and separate funding—their only commonality being their physical location.

In the late 1990s, the Pueblo City-County Library District in Colorado (www.pueblolibrary.org) realized it could no longer continue to fund its outreach services with a bookmobile. The library instead approached the school district with the idea of supplying library materials to be housed in the school buildings, with the public library maintaining a presence through these "satellite" libraries in elementary and middle schools.[6] If your community might be interested in creating a joint use library or a satellite system like the one in Pueblo County, consult the joint use bibliography of the American Library Association (ALA; www.ala.org/ala/aboutala/hqops/library/libraryfactsheet/alalibraryfactsheet20.cfm). Know the benefits as well as the drawbacks of this kind of collaborative project and use them to help you make an informed decision.

Statewide Collaborations

Collaborative projects between school and public libraries can be quite complex and involved on the local level, but they become even more complicated at the state level. A statewide initiative presents difficulties in terms of cost, the commitment required from individual communities, and differing population needs. Ideas also take time to develop. Often, when elected officials leave office, the plans leave with them—or their backers must start working with a new group of government officials.

If you do choose to work on a statewide collaboration, the place to start is with the existing associations in your area. Each state has its own library association; many offer grants and ideas for working with different community entities. Check to see if your school library media association is active in partnerships with any other organizations, or work directly with your state library. If you already have developed a positive partnership with your own school system and public library district, potential partners will see that you understand how to work toward a common goal and may be ready for more expansive projects. One such project in Illinois was the Reading to Learn conference, which was initiated by a community college library director. He saw a need for school administrators to recognize the importance of their school library media centers and to see them as more than just a space for computer labs (see the sidebar on page 88).

As with many great ideas, the problem of funding often gets in the way. In the Reading to Learn case, not long after the first conference had seen great success, the Illinois State Board of Education (ISBE) ran into serious financial trouble and was unable to meet its obligations. This put a strain on what had been promised to the attendees and forced the ultimate demise of the whole project. Although the conference was unable to attain its original goal of meeting for five years, it did result in some very positive outcomes. My own school district was lucky enough to participate in this conference, and the attending board member came away convinced that every school in our district needed to have a full-time school library media specialist on staff. The following year, the district hired two new librarians to meet this goal, which was a triumph for students and the district. More important, the school district has continued this commitment, staffing each new school built since the conference with a new school library media specialist.

Of course, statewide collaboration can be time consuming and costly and can involve a tremendous amount of effort. You may not have the time or energy to tackle these large-scale projects. But if you have an idea and think it is worthwhile as a state initiative, create a proposal and present it to relevant possible partners. You might be surprised by the welcome you receive, and the good that can be accomplished is measured in success stories like that of my own school district.

Reading to Learn

An interview with Eric Welch, dean, Learning Resources, 1986–2007, Highland Community College, Freeport, Illinois.

Q. How did the Reading to Learn Project begin?
A. When I was president of the Illinois Center for the Book, I met with Blouke and Marianne Carus, founders of Carus Publishing and publishers of *Cricket.* We discussed the disconnect that existed between libraries and schools. The Keith Curry Lance studies [mentioned in this book's Introduction] had shown a correlation between a strong and well-supported school library and academic achievement in schools. The Caruses and I wondered if there was not some way to convey this important message to school administrators.

I suggested the elements of what was to become the first Reading to Learn conference. A committee was formed by the Illinois Center for the Book to plan what became this conference. We made a presentation to the other partners, and there was widespread support for the idea. The idea was to bring together school administrators, school board members, librarians, and members of the community to hear how effective cooperation can achieve important student academic performance. (One suggestion for future improvement was that we include a teacher from the school.) The conference was kept very small, with no more than five teams, so that everyone could interact—and no one could skip out. One librarian remarked that it was the first time her administrator had been forced to participate in anything related to the library, and he went away impressed with the evidence of the link between strong libraries and general academic improvement schoolwide.

Q. Who were the main partners in the project?
A. Illinois Center for the Book, Carus Publishing and the Hegeler Carus Foundation, Highland Community College, Illinois State Board of Education (ISBE), and the Illinois State Library. We also received support from the Illinois State Library and Media Association. The Hegeler Carus Foundation and the Illinois State Library provided the main financial support. The ISBE had committed to financial support, but because of budgetary issues and the loss of staff, it was unable to meet its commitments.

Q. How was it decided to make this a statewide effort?
A. The idea was to include as disparate a group of schools as possible. There was an application process with commitments that had to be met. We wanted rural, inner city, and moderately supported school representation, but each had to agree to the minimum requirements. In fact, the Rockford School District called at the last minute to say its board member could not come. Because we believed that it was essential to the process to have board representation, it was eliminated from the group of schools.

Q. Could you please explain what the main goal(s) was/were of Reading to Learn?
A. The ultimate goal, of course, was to improve the academic performance of students in K–12. Another goal was to improve the visibility and importance of libraries in the K–12 environment at a time when the role of libraries is shifting and administrations tend to view the digitization of information as eliminating the need for libraries and librarians. The conference goal was to show how that view is a fallacious one and to build community support for libraries through the use of evidence and partnerships.

Q. Why was it deemed important to have a partner from out-side the school commit to the project, as well as the school district?

A. The idea was to create a partnership that would build a long-term relationship between the school, community, and public library, all in support of higher academic perform-ance. Ideally, the project would create an alliance among the community and school in support of higher academic stan-dards, making the library an integral component of that.

The failure of some of the partners to be able to continue to fund the project was a disappointment. This was intended to be a five-year initiative but lasted for only one, so there was no chance to do a long-term evaluation of the effects. In that sense, it did not meet the goals of the project. Evaluations from the participants in the first conference were very posi-tive, however, and all of the library representatives thanked the project planners for creating an environment where board and administrative representatives heard evidence of the academic benefits to having a strong and well-supported library in the K–12 environment. That was one of the goals that was indeed met.

It has always been my hope that the Illinois Community College association, NILRC, could make the linkage between high schools and community colleges a statewide effort and coordinate activities. To date, we have not been able to do this.

National Collaborations

Attempting collaboration on a national scale may sound like a deliberate plot to drive a librarian insane. Yet three groups of librarians have come together to create a fruitful national commit-tee through the ALA, proving that even the most daring of schemes can succeed. In 2003, a group of librarians realized just how much they could gain from working together through their various associations under the larger ALA umbrella. These three groups, the American Association of School Librarians (AASL), the Association for Library Service to Children (ALSC), and the Young Adult Library Services Association (YALSA), all had members interested in furthering services to the youth they interacted with. They saw collaboration between school and public libraries as a perfect melding of their efforts (see the sidebar on page 92).

The endeavors of the AASL/ALSC/YALSA Interdivisional Committee on School/Public Library Cooperation show how closely linked we truly are, whether we work in a public library or a school or whether we serve young children or teenagers. (Information on the extensive work of this committee can be found at www.ala.org/ala/mgrps/divs/aasl/aboutaasl/aaslgovernance/aaslcommittees/schoolpublic.cfm, and information on cooperative programs it has identified can be found at www.ala.org/ala/mgrps/divs/alsc/initiatives/partnerships/coopacts/school plcoopprogs.cfm.) We all have the same goals, and this committee gives us all more resources with which to engage in debate and tools with which to begin our own partnerships.

Take a Deep Breath

While the preceding sections were full of ideas and possibilities, remember to take only what you need now and save the rest for later. The possibilities for larger partnerships and collaborations can be overwhelming, but you have to begin somewhere—don't be discouraged by what others have already accomplished. What one has created, another can expand or adapt to fit her own situation. Not everyone is ready for a communitywide project or a statewide effort. However, there may come a day when this is the next ship you see on your horizon, so understand there will be others just waiting for you to join them on their collaborative journey.

Joining Ranks

An interview with Gail Bush, PhD, professor, and director, Center for Teaching Through Children's Books, National-Louis University, and AASL/ALSC/YALSA Joint Committee on School/Public Library Cooperation committee chair, 2007–2008.

Q. How was the idea for a joint task force of the American Association of School Librarians (AASL), the Association for Library Service to Children (ALSC), and Young Adult Library Services Association (YALSA) conceived?

A. The task force was the brainchild of Cynthia Richey, a past president of ALSC. Cynthia mentioned the idea in an article in the ALSC newsletter. Grace Shanahan then emailed Cynthia because it was exactly what Grace was working on in Brooklyn—developing cooperation between schools and the public libraries. The discussion led to the combined Youth Board meeting, and the rest is history.

Q. What was the charge of the task force?

A. To develop a signature project for the Youth Divisions regarding school/public library cooperative activities and create an action plan for the development of a product (e.g., programs, toolkit, website, clearinghouse for ideas about activities, programs, and services) that would draw attention to and promote best practices in school/public library cooperation. We expected the task force to look at local and national models of cooperative activities.

Q. How did the task force operate?

A. The task force members met at ALA annual and midwinter during the ALSC all-committee meeting time. Every meeting found members stepping up to assume responsibilities. Each one of us believed in our charge; we had a shared vision of serving our communities through cooperation and collaboration. Early in our meetings, we developed the "backscratcher" as our talisman. It stood for the cooperative nature of our charge—we scratch each other's backs. As chairperson, Grace ran an effective, friendly, and powerful meeting. Initially members from each of the three divisions posted queries to various local, state, and national listservs to gather activities from around the country. Jackie Partch (YALSA) did a yeoman's job of sorting the responses and then posting the exemplary projects and activities to the ALA website.

We all agreed that librarians would also learn from pitfalls and cautionary tales. Kate Todd (ALSC) updated her extensive bibliography and then posted it and links to related resources through various divisional (online) venues. Jami Jones (AASL) and I (AASL) began writing on behalf of the task force and published a column in *School Library Journal* and an article in *School Library Media Activities Monthly*. "Scratching Each Other's Library Backs: Best Practices on School/Public Library Cooperative Activities" was presented at concurrent sessions at the ALA in Chicago, AASL in Pittsburgh, and PLA in Boston conferences, with all members participating, including Kevin Scanlon (YALSA), Susan Hawk (YALSA), and Debbie McGuire (ALSC). We distributed colorful backscratchers to attendees at each program. We were delighted when ALSC president Ellen Fader joined our AASL presentation. Kate's PowerPoint presentation was outstanding (complete with animated backscratchers); we had panel presentations and interactive workshop activities for attendees. All members contributed to the Best Practices Checklist.

Q. What were the essential ingredients?

A. It is probably safe to say that the work of the task force could not have been accomplished without electronic communication. Considering that we actually met only twice a year for three years, we accomplished a tremendous amount. We all tried to attend the meetings consistently, but life gets in the way sometimes. Email was essential. Also disseminating our work easily through the ALA website fostered our clearinghouse role. The most essential ingredient was the participation and genuine interest of school and public librarians from around the country who contributed their projects and activities and attended our conference sessions. They were an enthusiastic and lively bunch and amazed us with their generosity.

Q. Why did the joint task force move to a formal committee?

A. Kate probably answered why we morphed into a committee best: "Almost every week on the pubyac listerv I see a query asking for advice on developing a cooperative school/public library program." The same is true from the school librarian viewpoint. We had unanimous support from all task force members. The work is not yet completed; we have barely opened the lines of communication between school and public librarians. We are all dedicated to serving youth, are overworked and underfunded. If we can learn from our colleagues because someone else has been there and done that before, it is worth the effort to make that connection. If we can serve our communities better and make libraries more meaningful to children and youth through cooperation, let's do it.

Our missions are served best through our shared vision. The charge of the committee is: "The AASL/ALSC/YALSA Interdivisional Committee on School/Public Library Cooperation will identify and disseminate information on effective cooperation or collaboration projects that link schools and public libraries. The committee will maintain and update the resources that have been compiled on the ALA website. The committee will develop training workshops and/or programs on cooperative or collaborative projects and present them at conferences, institutes, and for other organizations serving youth. Committee members will detail findings in articles or books for division publications." None of the task force members could have anticipated the depth of sharing or the collegiality that would be felt among the group. Our shared vision was tested and proven, and our many accomplishments tell the story of school and public librarians everywhere in America cooperating in innovative ways. Cooperation does not always have a price, but it does always make us feel richer for the experience.

Endnotes

1. Howard County Library, "A+ Partners in Education," www.hclibrary. org/index.php?page=13 (accessed June 13, 2008).
2. Multnomah County Library, "School Corps," www.multcolib.org/schoolcorps (accessed June 14, 2008).
3. Margaret Tice, "Queens Borough Public Library and the Connecting Libraries and Schools Project," *Journal of Youth Services in Libraries* 14:3 (2001): 11.
4. Tice, 11.
5. Alan Bundy and Larry Amey, "Libraries Like No Others: Evaluating the Performance and Progress of Joint Use Libraries," *Library Trends* 54:4 (2006): 501.
6. Richard Tucey and Carol Rooney, "The School/Public Library Alliance: The Pueblo Library District Experience," *Colorado Libraries* 25:1 (1999): 21.

Chapter 6

Using Technology to Partner

Libraries have always been more than mere book reposi-
tories. Their role as a place that is open to all community
members—regardless of race, gender, or socioeconomic
status—puts libraries in an ideal position to become
community hubs.

—*Meredith Farkas*[1]

We are all aware that times have changed. Whether you are a public librarian running storytimes for preschoolers or a school library
media specialist placed in charge of your school's computer network, technology affects what you are expected to work with and
how you interact with youth. For some, this can be daunting, confusing, and even scary, while others embrace technological challenges and bemoan the slowness of administrators and budgets to
keep up with the explosive pace of the digital world. Most of us fall
somewhere along this continuum, hoping for a happy medium of
progress and normalcy in order to be able to provide our services.

The vast array of technological possibilities available to us today
can be not only overwhelming but also confusing, because we
have to decide where to expend our time, energy, and precious
funds. We seem to face more demands on our time every day. Not
only do most librarians check voicemail, snail mail, and email on a
regular basis, but we also must keep up with lists, blogs, podcasts,
wikis, and other online resources and communities. It is no wonder time seems to pass ever faster; libraries need to be at the forefront of these technologies.

So where do partnership and collaboration enter into this picture, where time is of the essence and everyone seems to be
scrambling to meet the growing demands of the digital world?

Making technology work for your libraries builds on the same principles as other collaborative efforts and can save time and money in your partnership. Look at any project you begin in terms of where technology might appropriately fit in, helping to increase results and achieve your goals in a more efficient and timely fashion. Since many of us currently lack the know-how to best utilize this technology or are not fully aware of its potential and possibilities, this is another area where working in partnership can benefit us all. Your colleague might bring technical savvy to the partnership, while your skills may lie in marketing or fundraising; she might be a PowerPoint or MySpace expert, while you shine in working on a blog or wiki. Use each other's strengths and ideas in technology, as in all other areas of your collaboration.

Getting Started

Before beginning any collaborative project using technology, decide on what you hope to accomplish. When a new and exciting technological innovation comes along, sometimes we just want to try out the new tool, without considering whether it is the most appropriate approach for a given project. If exploring new technology is your passion, go for it—but you might want to hold off on inviting the other library to participate until you have worked out all the kinks and determined where the technology could benefit both libraries. On the flip side, if you really love working with new software, tools, and gadgets, make sure your counterpart across the way knows this. Maybe she is just dying to make a "Welcome to the Library" movie, for instance, but lacks the hardware, software, or know-how. Again, establishing a relationship and learning each other's strengths before embarking on any collaborative process is always beneficial.

Anytime you begin a collaborative process, consider if use of a given technology is essential—or just time consuming. Would a PowerPoint presentation to the PTA/PTO showing how its funds were used for a joint public/school library book club be impressive and informative? Sure. Is it worth your time and effort to produce the piece? Perhaps. Could this PowerPoint be used more than once? (For the teachers, the principal, the school board, the public library board?) The more potential uses for a finished product, the more it makes sense to invest your time in this endeavor. Consider the following points when contemplating using technology in your collaboration:

- Evaluate the nature of the project. Not every project lends itself to technology; in others, technological methods can complement other approaches. For example, a public librarian might produce a line of genre-centered book-talks on DVD and send copies to school libraries. Yet she also may still go into the schools to booktalk the con-tenders for the state's book competition. A large public library district that covers many schools might create a DVD highlighting the state book award titles, while in a smaller district, the children's librarian might visit the schools in person to help build relationships with the school library media specialist, teachers, and students.

- Be aware of your target audience. Younger audiences especially appreciate technology; teens in particular spend a lot of time in online communities and tend to make the most of new electronic resources quickly. Even very young children are being asked to show computer competency skills. If you use the same software and hard-ware they are expected to use, you reinforce the validity of the skill set they are learning.

- Consider the extra time needed to create something using technology. As much as we all like to believe that comput-ers save us time, just making a simple flyer can take hours if you can't get a text box to move to the right location. Nothing eats up your time like a software program that doesn't work the way you expect it to. Always double your time estimate, just to be on the safe side. As you grow more comfortable and gain experience working with a specific type of hardware or software, you will be better able to accurately predict your time frame.

- Examine your product and see how you can make it useful for the longest period of time and to the widest audience. The more uses for a project, the better your time is spent. Why create a movie, flyer, newsletter, or PowerPoint for just one group? Make it versatile to get more mileage out of your effort.

- Know your own comfort level with technology before attempting a project. Also find out if your partner is versed in the technologies you plan to use or perhaps would like to be. Tailoring your plans to your abilities can make the difference between getting your project in on time and never getting it off the ground. Admit when something is beyond your scope of expertise, and find someone to assist you in gaining the knowledge you need.

Technology can make a project, especially a presentation, "pop." Using digital video and images in presentations can create a huge visual impact and convey your ideas to a larger audience. People remember information better when they can see as well as hear it. Children and teens especially enjoy being visually stimulated, so use technology appropriately to maximize the impact of your collaborative project.

Communicating and Learning, Together

As mentioned earlier, taking the time to create, establish, and maintain relationships will aid you in your quest to develop collaborative partnerships with other libraries. Thanks to technology, it is easier than ever before to build relationships. You can quickly contact libraries in other districts, states—and even other countries. While most of us probably won't be reaching out to New Zealand for the latest information on booktalks, it's possible—and just might assist you in the long run. Finding ideas for collaborative projects and seeing what others are doing is where technology can really help your imagination take flight. A simple Internet search can lead you to a wealth of information and an instant shared community.

Connect on the Internet to find both new ideas and possible partners beyond your local area. Many librarians present at conferences, for instance, and will work collaboratively on a presentation with others even though they are many miles apart. There is no reason you can't take an idea you see on a California school library website and incorporate it into a partnership closer to your home in Mississippi. Many public libraries now post monthly calendars, and viewing just a few of these can get the creative juices flowing. Use all the wonderful social networking software the online world now provides at little or no cost to help you grow in your profession and your partnership.

Email Discussion Lists

You can find an email discussion list on just about every topic; not surprisingly, librarians have quite a few of their own. Many lists are sponsored through the American Library Association (ALA) and its subgroups, and most library associations and organizations host their own more specialized lists. Public librarians and school library media specialists have a number of different ALA lists to choose from—check out the directory of ALA mailing lists (lists.ala. org/sympa). Be aware that some of these require you to belong to both ALA and the sponsoring division or roundtable. Also check with your state library to see if there is a state-sponsored topical list for your area.

Start by investigating these popular lists:

- YALSA Young Adult Advisory Councils (lists.ala.org/sympa/info/ya-yaac) – A great resource for seeing what programs are popular with teens and determining if these could be used cooperatively with another library.

- YALSA Book Discussions (lists.ala.org/sympa/info/yalsa-bk) – Incredibly useful for any questions relating to books, including ideas for booktalks, book discussion groups, and ideas for purchasing. Questions about collaboration often crop up on this list.

- Association for Library Service to Children (ALSC) List (lists.ala.org/sympa/info/alsc-l) – If you are working with younger students, a great place to get ideas for possible projects.

- ALSC Public Library–School Partnership Discussion List (lists.ala.org/sympa/info/alscpubsch) – *The* list for school/public library partnerships. Discussions are informative, and it's a great place to start asking questions before embarking on a collaborative effort.

- American Association of School Librarians (AASL) Members Forum (lists.ala.org/sympa/subscribe/aaslforum) – A good list for public librarians to check out as well, to help them understand some of the issues facing school librarians.

- LM_NET: Where School Librarians Connect (www.eduref.org/lm_net) – This fantastic list is wonderful for learning about real-life situations occurring in the schools.

- Illinois School Library Media Association (ISLMA) ISLMANET-L (www.islma.org/listserv.htm) – Geared for school library media specialists in Illinois but open to anyone; gives a great view into school life. Its members are eager to share stories and assist with problems and questions about collaboration between school and public libraries.

Probably the best way to find out about pertinent lists is by asking fellow colleagues. The web page for a list generally provides clear instructions on how to join and how to unsubscribe, and guidelines regarding what types of posts are allowed. School librarians might need to subscribe to these mailing lists using a personal email account, if their school account blocks list emails. You might want to set up a separate account just for list email or to filter list messages into folders on arrival, since some are quite busy and generate many messages each day. It can be difficult to wade through your inbox looking for a time-sensitive message lost among hundreds of posts discussing the latest movie based on a children's book.

Although most librarians currently belong to at least one list, this might not seem like a logical place to begin collaborative work, given the distances separating list participants. Actually, however, lists are the perfect place to begin contemplating partnerships and getting ideas:

- Lists are generally current and fast paced. Reading and participating let you keep your finger on the pulse of your area of interest.

- By their very nature, people involved in lists want to impart what they know to others. They want to learn about new trends and are interested in what is coming up next. A list is a wonderful place to explore an idea for a collaborative project, judge its plausibility by the feedback you receive from the group, and get thoughts on how best to proceed.

- Often, lists have archives where you can browse or search older posts. This lets you get a feel for the group in general and see if there are topics you can incorporate into one of your projects.

- Especially on a local list, there is a chance you will actually "bump into" someone in your general vicinity who shares your interests. This person may become a partner or give you advice on future collaborative projects.

When you are looking to build collaborative relationships, it is amazing where promising partners may appear.

Online Communities

As more people meet and connect online, communities are emerging around their common interests. Not only are people exchanging ideas and information online, they are creating lasting relationships as well. In these communities, you and your local partner(s) can exchange ideas with other librarians, gain experience working together, create online communities for the population you serve, and formulate goals and visions. As Meredith Farkas explains: "Libraries can use social software to build community with their web presence. A library's online presence can become a community forum, a space to share ideas, and a place where community members can connect with one another. Learning from existing online communities, libraries can find ways to connect with their patrons and develop online communities of their own, providing a vital online resource."[2]

Online communities consist of a group of individuals with a common interest or purpose, which works out wonderfully for librarians. How can school library media specialists and public librarians work together to create an online community for themselves or for their patrons? This might be as easy as creating a joint photo sharing account on Flickr (www.flickr.com) designed to support the local manga club and allowing students to view each other's works. By their very nature, blogs, nings, discussion groups, and forums lend themselves to a collaborative atmosphere; free online tools allow just about anyone to set these up. Ways to utilize some of these spaces will be discussed in more detail later in this chapter.

Blogs

Feel like sharing something? Anything? A blog on the subject probably already exists. Librarians love their blogs and love reading others'. Just what is a blog, and what makes blogs so popular? A blog is simply a website that shows posts, or updates, in reverse chronological order, and provides an easy-to-use interface that the blog author can use to create posts without any knowledge of HTML. Blogs can serve a variety of purposes, from chronicling the life of a small child to reflecting on the ins and outs of a given profession; they tend to be opinionated by their very nature. Blogs can incite some great discussions.

For a sampling of libraryland blogs, just go to Google, type in "library blogs," and hold on! If you prefer a somewhat more refined approach, find extensive lists of school and public library blogs at the Blogging Libraries Wiki (www.blogwithoutalibrary.net/links/index.php?title=Welcome_to_the_Blogging_Libraries_Wiki). A good example of a fun blog created by a school librarian is To Read or Not to Read (www.librarygoddess.blogspot.com); the author reviews young adult literature and rates the books. The possibilities for school and public library blogs are limited only by your imagination and time. Examples of how to use blogs in collaborative projects can be found later in this chapter.

If you are new to blogging, start with a hosted service such as Blogger (www.blogger.com) or WordPress (www.wordpress.com). Take the time to read some library-related blogs to get a feel for blogging and what you might incorporate if you decide to create a blog in partnership with another library. Kids love technology, and blogs are a great way to get them involved, either as contributors or commenters. Solicit students' help to maintain your blog; perhaps even make it a student-run project.

Wikis

Many school library media specialists already successfully use wikis on a daily basis to collaborate with students and teachers. According to Meredith G. Farkas, "Wikis give everyone the ability to take part in creating and editing web content. With simplified, easy-to-learn text-formatting rules, wikis truly put experienced Web designers and web novices on an equal footing."[3] Wikis allow a group of individuals to jointly create and edit a website by adding and subtracting content. This gives everyone a share in the site's design, concept, and purpose and offers the possibility of constant change.[4] This is the reason wikis are so appealing in the education field; they allow teachers to change assignments to meet new curriculum challenges, and they engage students to work collectively "to pool their research and analyze their data, forming a kind of understanding that would be difficult for an individual student to achieve."[5] They also enable a whole host of potential collaborations between school library media specialists and their colleagues.

A wiki may be the best choice for collaboration between librarians who are very busy and don't have the chance to connect on the phone, in person, or even by email on a regular basis. Since the wiki remains the same until someone changes it, and you control who has access, project ideas can be shared when you have the time to work on them, rather than on demand. You can focus on your plan when you have time and can elaborate on or add ideas when they occur to you, rather than shooting off an email, which might get lost in your partner's inbox. One bonus of a wiki is that as you work, you are creating a website about your project, where patrons and students can access information pertaining to the project once you have launched it. (Find more ideas on employing wikis in the section on using Web 2.0 tools to collaborate, later in this chapter.)

If you are new to wikis and looking to experiment, try one of these popular sites: Pbwiki (pbwiki.com), Wikispaces (www.wiki spaces.com), or Wetpaint (www.wetpaint.com). To get a feel for how wikis can be used, visit sites like WebTools4U2Use (webtools4u2use.wikispaces.com), which is aimed at school library media specialists but could be used by both public and school librarians to get a sense of what is possible. Also, don't miss Library Success: A Best Practices Wiki (www.libsuccess.org), which is a one-stop shop for sharing ideas and information on programs and technological innovations. Knowing how to use technology to stay connected, focused, and aware of your goals will help you be a better partner and allow the possibility for greater collaborations.

Share your observations with other librarians you are working with, and seek their knowledge in areas you are less familiar with.

Instant Messaging

Teens spend a lot of time both sending mobile text messages and "chatting" online. This real-time communication has become so popular that most tend to take it for granted these days. Many public libraries now offer services where patrons can ask questions via instant messaging (IM), using AOL Instant Messenger (AIM), Yahoo! Messenger, and MSN Messenger. Multiprotocol clients such as Trillian (www.ceruleanstudios. com) and online services such as Meebo (www.meebo.com) allow libraries to reach customers no matter which service they are using. Connecting with people by using a medium they are familiar and comfortable with just makes sense. Younger patrons especially tend to utilize these services and can help libraries push the envelope in offering nontraditional methods of information delivery.

So how can librarians benefit from using IM? The beauty of IM is that it lets you see when someone is online and available and allows for the free and immediate exchange of information, which is not always the case with other forms of communication such as email or telephone. Perhaps your school library is full of students, and your phone is in the back room. Or you are at the reference desk at the public library and have to stay off the phone and be available to customers. IM software lets you see if your partner is online, allowing you to stay connected, assist each other when necessary, and take your communication to another level. It also lets you jot a quick note or send an idea as it crosses your mind, rather than waiting and perhaps forgetting your flash of brilliance by the time you get a chance to sit down and type an entire email message or pick up the phone. The more access you have, the better the chances you will connect professionally—and perhaps personally.

Using Web 2.0 Tools to Collaborate

Most of us use online tools throughout our everyday lives; we don't hesitate to check our email, read a blog, or add to our MySpace page during our workday. These Web 2.0 tools, which allow us to interact, participate, and contribute online, have become so ingrained in our lives that we can't remember how we got along without them. Judy Hauser explains that: "Web 2.0 refers to the current web, an environment filled with opportunities to not only create content in new ways but also to share information, communicate differently, collaborate easily with the rest of the world and self-publish."[6] Using Web 2.0 technologies to bring libraries into a closer working relationship just makes sense. So how exactly can we use these tools and the concept of Web 2.0 to work in partnership with another library? Realize that schools often have restrictions on how Internet access can be used, as do some public libraries. These limitations may affect what you can achieve and the tools you can use. Some institutions, for example, block MySpace and other social sites, while others filter popular blogging sites. Be aware of any such restrictions in your or your partner's environment before launching a Web 2.0 project.

Blog and Wiki Potential

As mentioned earlier, wikis are wonderful tools for the joint creation of an easily edited work in progress. By their very nature, they lend themselves to collaboration. While many school library media specialists use wikis in their schools for brainstorming, book discussions, and writing lesson plans,[7] public librarians may not immediately see as many uses. However, the same cannot be said of blogs, which many public libraries currently maintain. Often written by the library director, these are usually intended to inform patrons and community members of the library's activities and future plans.

To determine if a wiki or blog might be a good way to partner, first examine how you currently use these resources. If your institution has already launched a blog and/or wiki, you may already have the perfect avenue to begin extending your services; if not, investigate some of the previously mentioned free resources to get started. School library media specialists can consider the following ideas for collaborating with blogs or wikis:

- Use wikis to create assignments that engage students in the learning and research process. For example, choose a historical period, have students record on the wiki as much information as they can uncover on the topic, and then have them read a historical novel set in the same period. Invite the public librarian to work with students on the joint wiki; ask her to comment on their work, suggest other resources to consider, and recommend appropriate historical novels. Open any wiki used for student assignments to your public librarian so she can contribute to the learning process.

- Work with teachers on a wiki to create ideas for lesson plans. Once again, give the public librarian access so that the public library can step in to offer support in areas where the school library may be weaker.

- Host blog-based book discussions for students and/or staff, and get the public librarian involved. Most public libraries have more funds available for purchasing print materials than school libraries. In addition, many public libraries now offer access to ebooks, which could be used by students as well as by the school library media center.

This kind of cooperative support tends to be nonthreatening, and using existing services requires a smaller time commitment.

Similarly, public librarians can reflect on ways to expand their blogs or wikis to give input to school library media specialists:

- Set aside a space for a book discussion blog, and then invite librarians from each of the schools the public library serves. Create a spot for school library media specialists to report on the "hottest" book in their schools each month; see if you can get a debate going about why certain books are more popular in one school than another. Also allow students to post comments; soliciting their participation will help them feel ownership of the blog and cultivate their information literacy skills.

- Publicize your blog to the school library media specialists. Encourage them to post when, for example, they see a need to expand the public library collection in a specific curriculum-related area and also to contribute any other observations they may have.

- Realize that your blog could be a fantastic way for school library media specialists to keep abreast of library activities available for their students. Make sure your events blog is updated in a timely fashion so that it becomes a reliable source of information for potential participants.

- Use a wiki to collect links to ready reference resources on both frequently asked reference questions and frequently assigned homework topics; ask the school librarian to contribute additional resources to curriculum-related sections.

Any of these activities help you keep each other informed and let you interact through established links. Expand your network of contacts, and you may discover new opportunities for collaboration. The more conversation that occurs, the more comfortable everyone will be when possible projects present themselves. Once you and a partner are both relaxed about using existing blogs and wikis, think of collaborating to create new ones that benefit both clienteles.

Ideas for Collaborative Projects
Using Web 2.0 Tools

- Create a joint school/public library discussion blog in which each librarian contributes titles, questions, and opinions on a regular basis.

- Encourage students to experiment with wiki tools to make a teen library page for the public library. Launch the site during Teen Read Week in October.

- Establish a student-directed blog on books, music, games, and other areas of interest to students, one for each grade level in your area of service.

- Use a MySpace page, wiki, or blog to highlight students' creative works, such as artwork, music, and literature. This site could be hosted by the public library or by a specific school, but still accept contributions from the whole school or public library district.

- Invite tech-savvy youth in your school or public library to form a group that will maintain and suggest material for a MySpace page. Invite students from different schools to broaden the relevance and appeal of the page.

- Create a series of library-related video clips to broadcast on YouTube. These can promote summer reading programs or contain booktalks, library instruction, or informative pieces for teachers or students (such as a presentation on copyright and fair use).

- Start a podcast with students. Have them record booktalks on a monthly basis. This series can be hosted at either the public library or the school library; share the technology needs and the credit.

MySpace, Their World

Anyone who is anyone has a MySpace page these days. Many public libraries have jumped on this bandwagon, especially to connect with their teen patrons and keep libraries relevant in their lives. Creating a MySpace page for your library is one way of going where the teens tend to be. School libraries are also starting to see the benefits of participating in this medium.

Check the following libraries' MySpace pages for examples of what libraries have done with their MySpace presence:

- Fountaindale Public Library, Bolingbrook, Illinois, profile.myspace.com/index.cfm?fuseaction=user. viewprofile&friendID=186861188

- Denver (CO) Public Library, www.myspace.com/denver_evolver

- Public Library of Charlotte and Mecklenburg County (NC), www.myspace.com/libraryloft

You can easily link to other MySpace pages and have them featured as "friends" on your own MySpace page. Link to author pages from your library's MySpace page so students can connect on a more personal level with the authors of books they enjoy and establish a link beyond the written page. Getting students engaged in what they read enables growth.

MySpace pages, though, can take longer to create and update than you might first think. (After all, every teenager seems to have one, so how hard could it really be?) You can find many helpful sites to assist MySpace beginners, such as CoolChaser (www.coolchaser.com), Free Web Layouts (www.freeweblayouts. net), and ProfileMods (www.profilemods.com). Your best resource, though, will be the people you serve. Teens can be invaluable in helping create a MySpace page. After all, they know what is cutting edge—and probably have already worked out the kinks on their own pages. Not only does it take time to create a page, but keeping it relevant will take time as well. As with a blog, it is important to change the information displayed on your MySpace page regularly, if possible. How frequently depends on your goals; if you simply want to display flyers on programs at the public library, you might need to update it less often.

Working jointly on a MySpace page first requires determining its purpose. Do you want to have a space where each library recommends books that are popular, new titles, and perhaps links to some literary friends? Will you incorporate a blog into the page—and if so, who will be responsible for updating it? Who are you trying to reach, and why do you want them to visit your page? Before engaging in this type of partnership, establish clear guidelines for who will add material, what the content will encompass, and how often new information will be added. Decide who will be responsible for viewing the posts and adding them to the space, and negotiate any controls and limits you want built into your page.

Check with other libraries in your area and see what they have done in this space. Ask how much time it takes to create and maintain their page. This page could be up for years—are you prepared to post to a MySpace blog once a week for years? How will you end the site gracefully, if it becomes too much of a burden to maintain? Could it be turned over to students, patrons, or colleagues without much difficulty? After these decisions have been made, it will be easier to determine whether you want to embark on a MySpace page collaboration with another library.

YouTube, Podcasts, and Beyond

If you need a video clip on any subject, someone has posted one on YouTube. Podcasts also abound on the web, on anything from parenting to favorite manga titles, and more people every day are deciding to try this form of communication on their own. With the current push for students to become information literate, it is little wonder these venues are being explored by school library media specialists as well as public librarians. How, then, can these wonderful tools be used most effectively as part of the collaborative process?

The possibilities for these tools are limited only by your imagination, knowledge, and the technology available in your facility. Take a few minutes to explore YouTube with a search as vague as "public libraries." You'll see everything from a day in the life of a library to entries for library film festivals to bookcart drill team competitions. The sky is the limit, and you can use others' videos to inspire your own ideas. Perhaps the hardest part of venturing into this arena will be deciding which ideas you want to try on your own and which would work best in a partnership.

One project that lends itself well to YouTube is a film festival for students. Use the public library to do a big screening. Then, post the submissions on YouTube to allow greater access to these movies; allow viewers to vote on their favorites. Alternatively, why not have students experience the process of creating and casting a television show? Have students vie to create the premise of the show by submitting scripts on your MySpace page, blog, or wiki, and let their peers vote to pick the best one. Then, have an online casting call—all students who want to be in the show would have to post a video audition tape on YouTube so that the director and others could view the potential participants.

When libraries work together, rather than limiting a competition to just one school, more students have a chance to participate. Teachers can work a project like this into the curriculum, possibly in terms of learning computer skills, public speaking, or writing. Each episode of the show could be written collaboratively on a wiki, perhaps with a different class or group taking responsibility for each episode. The final episode could be shot on location at one of the participating schools or the public library. Obviously, this would be a long-term, intensive project. The concept shows, though, how Web 2.0 tools can easily be used to create something the students would thoroughly enjoy—while giving them valuable instruction in the process. Who better to make technology relevant and fun than the librarians in their lives?

Podcasting takes the idea of posting a single video to YouTube a bit further, by actually creating an ongoing program. As Linda

Braun notes in her book, *Listen Up! Podcasting for Schools and Libraries*, a podcast can contain either video or audio content.[8] Both audio and video podcasts can be targeted to a particular audience. For example, you could focus your podcast on the services you have available to just sixth graders or to English teachers or to fantasy readers. For a great step-by-step guide on how to launch your own podcast—and get others to listen to it—Braun's book is the place to start. Here are some ideas for jointly created podcasts:

- Target new teachers. Show them how both the public library and school library media center can assist them. Podcasts could include information on obtaining a teacher card, borrowing materials from the public library, and using interlibrary loan. You could also include instruction on using library databases and information on school district policies. Interview veteran teachers and ask them for some examples of how teachers might collaborate with the school library media specialist on the curriculum.

- Create a podcast on new books for students and teachers. Highlight a variety of titles to make this germane to a larger audience.

- Create single podcasts that focus on specific curriculum needs, such as the Holocaust, state award books, Westward Expansion, or Newbery winners. You can add a few of these each year, giving teachers a simple way to introduce a unit of study.

- Generate podcasts of booktalks created by students, for students. Use these as a way to promote literacy.

- Use podcasts to inform staff in the other institution about relevant news and developments in your library.

Into Cyberspace

An interview with Kelly Czarnecki, Technology Education Librarian at ImaginOn, Public Library of Charlotte and Mecklenburg County (NC).

Q. Could you describe how you came to utilize Web 2.0 tools in your position? And how has that changed (if it has) how you interact with your client/patron base?
A. I have been using Web 2.0 tools such as wikis and Google Docs (docs.google.com) for a while with my colleagues to get work done and share information. It seemed just as natural to use tools such as YouTube with patrons, since we promote and offer movie, gaming, and music creation programs in the library.

Q. How do you see Web 2.0 tools changing the face of librarianship (or has it already changed), and what possibilities do you see for the future?
A. I see these tools changing business in general, bringing forth the stories and conversations of our patrons/users/customers, which is exactly what libraries are all about. I think using these tools has a way to go, in terms of a profession needing to be, not information experts, but guides to information—who can welcome and incorporate the knowledge our users have. Possibilities for the future: I see us as getting smarter the more we're open to collaborating.

Q. Do you feel these tools make collaboration easier in general? Examples?
A. Yes, definitely, because these tools help create relationships that are much more fluid than those that would exist without them. In using Twitter (www.twitter.com), for example, it's easy to share byte-sized chunks of information on the

go from a phone or computer. This allows for that spontaneous kind of resource sharing.

Q. Have you collaborated/partnered with school libraries in your capacity? If so, what were the results, and what tools did you use during this partnership?
A. Yes, I used to booktalk from the public library with the school librarian, and we started to create podcasts with Audacity (audacity.sourceforge.net) to interest the teens in books. I think this helped reach teens outside of the classroom and outside of the library's collection.

Q. What opportunities for collaboration with school libraries do you see in the future, considering the technology that is present and might be around the corner?
A. I think Second Life (www.secondlife.com) is one example that uses a lot of the Web 2.0 tools available (Twitter, Moodle, profiles, IM, video creation and editing) and is a place where school and public libraries can easily interact with each other.

Q. Please explain what Teen Second Life is, your role in creating it, and how teenagers are connecting with libraries through this medium.
A. Teen Second Life (teen.secondlife.com) is a 3D virtual world created by its residents, ages 13–17. Adults have access to the teen grid, as long as they have passed a background check; there are over 45 adult-owned islands on the teen grid. My role is that I own an island on the grid, Eye4You, which is sponsored by my public library in real life.

In answer to how teens are connecting with libraries through this medium, I feel that this question looks at the library as a physical place. There *are* ways that teens are connecting with libraries as a physical place (i.e., going to their local library and accessing Teen Second Life)—but, more important to me, the participation of a library or librarian in Teen Second Life can help teens connect with the *values* of a library. Even if a library or librarian is not involved in Teen Second Life, the 3D platform itself is chock full of opportunities to better understand the facets of media literacy—which are tools we all need in this tech-savvy environment. Teen Second Life encourages collective intelligence. It's an inherently social platform where conversation and creation and ownership of knowledge are at the forefront. For example, the teens on Eye4You are constructing a medieval village. They learned through each other the characteristics of the time period and how to construct a 3D model of it. This employed their judgment of what to use and not to use—which is part of information literacy.

Podcasting seems tailor made for collaboration. After all, if you plan on a series of podcasts, it always helps to have more than one person providing material, rounding up interviewees, and coming up with ideas for future episodes. If you currently produce a podcast, consider opening it up to your counterpart at the other library. You might be surprised how much that person can add to your program.

Some libraries are already going beyond wikis, blogs, and MySpace pages. Each library has its own pace of technological development; while some may shuffle along, others are blazing ahead and creating new and exciting developments for everyone. Kelly Czarnecki (see sidebar on page 116) is one such leader. With her support, teenagers have gained a voice and a space in the 3D virtual world of Teen Second Life. Here people meet and discuss, roleplay, and work together to create a world in cyberspace. Czarnecki sees many such ways for libraries to use technology to bring youth into their world, including virtual bookmaking using programs like Photoshop and sites like Flickr, and interpretation of events through 3D simulations and/or role-playing. All of these activities can involve research, and therefore the library's resources. Talking with others in the field, attending conferences, and reading the literature let you stay current on these exciting new developments and give you more ideas about where you can use this fabulous technology to partner.

Endnotes

1. Meredith Farkas, *Social Software in Libraries: Building Collaboration, Communication, and Community Online* (Medford, NJ: Information Today, Inc., 2007), 85.
2. Farkas, 85.
3. Farkas, 67.
4. Farkas, 68.
5. Doug Achterman, "Beyond Wikipedia," *Teacher Librarian* 34:2 (2006): 19.
6. Judy Hauser, "Media Specialists Can Learn Web 2.0 Tools to Make Schools More Cool," *Computers in Libraries* 27:2 (2007): 7.
7. Hauser, 8.
8. Linda Braun, *Listen Up! Podcasting for Schools and Libraries* (Medford, NJ: Information Today, Inc., 2007), xv.

Chapter 7

Resource Sharing

A common concern in all types of libraries is the lack of sufficient funding for both print materials and electronic resources. Each library faces its own challenges, and most are under pressure to meet the demands of their constituencies by doing more with less. Realize, though, that this situation provides the perfect landscape for developing additional ties between school and public libraries. A chance to stretch limited funding can make the most apprehensive administrator pay attention to the possibilities of collaboration.

Resource sharing can be as easy as having a public librarian pull books for the school library media specialist or as complicated as establishing a schedule for students to visit the public library's bookmobile every month. As with all things collaborative, focus on what will work best for both situations and both libraries. This will assist you in deciding the level of commitment needed to share your valuable resources.

It's All About the Books

When I was working as a young adult librarian, one of the middle schools in our district had a flood that basically destroyed the school library media center and most of its contents. While the school district allocated funds to buy new books, anyone who has seen an opening-day collection can attest that the shelves still looked pretty bare. At the time, I was in the process of weeding the young adult collection at the public library. I asked the school library media specialist if she would be interested in some of the nicer withdrawn books, which I had weeded due to low circulation and lack of space. She was very happy to receive them, so over the next few years, anytime I had some books in good shape that I couldn't keep, I passed them along to her. This took little effort on my part—and looking back, I wish I'd thought to do more to get materials into that library.

However, this partnership did help get additional books on the shelves and into the hands of students in our district. We were sharing resources by redistributing them. (Of course, this is not to say that all school library media specialists would want withdrawn public library books, or that all public libraries are even allowed to "redistribute" their withdrawn books.) But our unique circumstances, as well as the fact that both parties were open to the idea, allowed this sharing to succeed. As always, consider your own needs and those of the other library, and how you can best address them. Sharing resources can sometimes be the best solution.

Interlibrary Loan Service

One of the remarkable functions of libraries is that they lend their books out to just about anyone, anywhere! When I first learned about interlibrary loan (ILL), I was very impressed. Basically, ask for a book, and you shall receive. This really is an incredible service, but not everyone uses it, or even knows it exists. Even librarians sometimes fail to take advantage of the service. Most school library media specialists are aware of ILL, but they may not utilize it because they lack the time, technology, or understanding of the specifics. Public librarians may likewise underutilize ILL, especially at a larger institution, because departments are more specialized and they simply might not think of the service if they don't use it on a regular basis. Whatever your situation, you can find ways to use ILL to benefit your patrons and expand your collection.

Public librarians should make sure the school library media specialists in their district are aware of ILL and its potential benefits for them. Present this information at a meeting of the school library media specialists; show them how they can submit an ILL request. Give practical examples, such as using ILL to request materials to supplement a teacher's knowledge of a specific subject (e.g., a book with copies of primary sources from the Civil War). Outline the responsibilities involved in ILL; explain how books need to be returned and what, if any, penalties will be incurred if they are late or lost. Most important, show how just having this service available increases their collections exponentially.

If you are a school library media specialist, make sure you know how to place holds and receive requested items. If you live in a more rural area, your larger county library system may be able to assist you if your local public library is unable to. Or check with the next largest public library in your area. Even if it doesn't directly serve your school district, it may be able to give you the information you need to get started. Make your teachers aware of ILL so that they know they can request books or DVDs to supplement the curriculum. Even if this is not a service schools need on a day-to-day basis, it can be quite useful to school librarians and teachers.

Typically, most ILL transactions between school and public libraries involve a school requesting materials from the public library, rather than the public library asking for books from a school, for two reasons. School libraries may not have their online catalog linked to the outside world, so people cannot see what is in the collection. Also, school library collections tend to be smaller and curriculum-specific; thus they are less likely to have what a public library patron is seeking.

Off the Shelves, Into the Classrooms

Many of us librarians, both school and public, struggle daily with the best ways to effectively reach our audience. This is where a school library media specialist has an advantage over a public librarian: She has built-in proximity. Knowing this, it makes sense for public librarians to reach out to share their materials with school library media specialists, who can get the materials into the hands of their mutual audience. There are several simple yet effective ways of moving books and other resources to where they can be most valuable.

Many public libraries are happy to pull a selection of books on a given topic for a school library media specialist or a teacher and either set them aside for in-library student use or loan the whole batch to the school. This is an easy way to expand the resources of the school library media center with little effort, as well as to increase circulation of the public library's collection. This simple service allows librarians to enrich the school's curriculum without additional expense, and it works to everyone's advantage. When employing this service, keep the following issues in mind:

- Timing – School library media specialists should be sure to leave adequate time for the public library to fill your request. Requesting books the same day they are needed puts undue stress on everyone. Try to impress this upon your teachers, as well!

- Collection size – Public librarians should inform school library media specialists if their requests are difficult to fill or may inconvenience other patrons. For example, a history teacher may want 25 sixth-grade-level books on the Civil War. The public library may not realistically be able to fill this kind of order, depending on the size of its collection.

- Repeat requests – Both public and school librarians should keep track of repeat requests and anticipate recurring needs. For example, if second-grade students in your district always study "insects with wings" in April, the public librarian should make note of this and be prepared; if the public library orders more books on this topic, this information can be forwarded to the school library media specialist. Conversely, if the curriculum changes, and second graders no longer study winged insects—but fourth graders do—the school library media specialist needs to inform the public librarian. This allows her to let the school know what is available for that level and to shift the grade level of her purchases on that subject.

- Overuse – Excessive use of this service can wear down those filling the orders. If a school requests an abundance of materials on a weekly basis, it might be time to sit down with the school library media specialist and principal to see if more funds could be allocated for the school library media center. The public librarian should keep track of the requests and number of items pulled, which will give the school library media specialist ammunition in justifying additional funding for the school library.

- Curriculum alignment – Obviously, the school library media center needs to align its collection with the curriculum. However, it never hurts for the public library also to be aware of the assignments coming through its doors; school library media specialists should share the district curriculum with the public library, and public librarians should ask to see a copy. Having this information helps public libraries ensure that their collections meet the needs of students who visit the public library and highlights any gaps.

When both parties are considerate of each other's needs, pulling materials for teachers can be an extremely productive use of the public library's resources. This service expands the available resources for students and benefits everyone.

Some public libraries have created "bags-o-books," which are specifically targeted to younger grade levels. These thematic bags often include not only books but also DVDs, puppets, and other resources pertaining to a particular topic. The whole package can then be checked out as a single item by a teacher or school library media specialist. If your public library does not currently offer this service, consult with the school library media specialists to see

Establishing Parameters

Loaning books or other materials from the public library to the school may seem simple, but consider the following questions before you embark on this service:

- Who will be the contact person/people at the public library? Who will make requests from the schools? Will teachers call in their own requests, or will these be filtered through the school library media specialist? Will all requests go through the public library's children's department, young adult department, or adult/ reference department? Will this depend on the grade level of the materials being requested?
- If the materials are intended for in-school use, who will pick them up? Is a courier available to run books between the public library and the schools, or will transporting materials be the responsibility of the school librarian? The young adult librarian? How long will the public library hold materials before putting them back into circulation?
- Will materials going to the schools be checked out under the school library media specialist's name or the teacher's?
- Who will take responsibility for renewing the materials if they are needed for longer than the usual checkout period?
- What will happen if materials are late or lost? Will there be a charge? Who will pay?

Knowing the answers to these questions in advance will alleviate some pitfalls of loaning materials from the public library to the school.

what topics might appeal to the teachers and create some bags. Publicize the availability of these materials to the schools so that teachers and the school librarians are aware of the convenience of bagged materials to support the curriculum.

Creating Partnerships Through Book Exchanges

When I worked at a public library, I often found myself scrambling to spend hundreds of dollars at the last minute. Our fiscal year ended in June, and in order to get all the processing done on time, we had to stop ordering by the end of April. At crunch time each year, I would be poring over journals and catalogs, furiously adding to my Baker & Taylor cart. I always wanted to use these funds to purchase class sets for the public schools to check out. (Class sets provide each student in the class, or each of a small group of students within the class, with a copy of a given book.) Not only would our circulation statistics have increased when a teacher used a set, but our library could have infused much-needed new life to our school district's anemic approved reading lists and publicized how the public library was assisting the schools. Unfortunately, I was unable to get approval for this idea—but I never forgot it.

Fortunately, many public libraries do see the wisdom in offering class sets to the school districts they serve. You may decide you would like to begin this service at your public library, or a school library media specialist could suggest his local public library begin providing it. (Remember to stress those circulation statistics!) Both libraries need to establish what will happen in the case of lost or damaged books. The school librarian should reassure the public library that he is aware the school is using the public library's money and that he appreciates its assistance to the school library and the students.

Depending on the school district and its curriculum, some schools maintain extensive lists of books from which teachers can select their classroom reading sets. These lists are usually approved by a group consisting of teachers, school library media specialists, and perhaps parents, as well as the school board, and are vetted for content and appropriate age levels. School library media specialists should be aware of this selection process and make every attempt to be included on the committee that decides what titles will be added or reevaluated. Public librarians should find out who makes these kinds of decisions in their district schools and see if they can have some kind of input. After all, public librarians read a tremendous amount of material each year and generally have a much larger, broader collection than the school libraries. You should be able to contribute to the dialogue on what materials would benefit students.

Typically, school lists are broken down by grade level. This allows teachers to see what books students may already have read in previous grades. In theory, it also keeps a fourth-grade teacher from teaching *Tuck Everlasting* when the committee has determined that this book is more appropriate for sixth grade. In some districts, teachers are limited to using books on the approved list; in others, they are allowed to choose alternate materials for their classes. While the list itself may be extensive, the actual number of full class sets available might be very limited—and the condition of the books fairly miserable. Here is where the school library media specialist and the public librarian can work together to ensure students and teachers have access to relevant and meaningful reading material.

Each year, set aside time to meet with the English teachers in local secondary schools and the elementary teachers at each grade level. Obviously, if you work in a large school district, getting to see each teacher in person would be time consuming—or impossible. This is where email lists and some of the other techniques discussed in Chapter 6 can come in handy. Communicate with teachers via your blog or a newsletter; let them know that you are interested in finding out what titles they would like to teach using class sets. Keep in mind that not all teachers are avid readers, and they might appreciate having some information about each book on the list before making a selection.

An informal informational meeting is an excellent way to help teachers make a knowledgeable decision on new titles for class sets. School librarians and public library school services coordinators could cohost an afternoon tea at the public library and take turns booktalking selections from the list. Even if only a few teachers attend, they will talk to their colleagues and spread information about these materials. Include a variety of both fiction and nonfiction books. You can also think outside the approved list; find a few new titles that most of you agree would be suitable, and booktalk those as well. It doesn't hurt to get people thinking about expanding the list for next year. After all, the more choices teachers have, the more likely they will be to find a book that resonates with them personally. As we all know, if you love what you are teaching, your enthusiasm is infectious.

Once staff have pared the list down to several contenders, you might want to poll the students. Booktalk these titles to students in the school library, on lunch breaks, or during scheduled class times. You might use voting privileges as an incentive for good behavior, such as returning books on time (any class that returns all its books on time during a certain time frame gets to participate in the vote). Make this a fun chance for students to decide on what they would like to read as a class, together.

Also check to see if the public library already purchases multiple copies of titles for statewide reading competitions in which students vote for their favorite book (see Chapter 2). Often a public library will purchase as many as 10 copies of such books to meet demand, but once the competition has passed, they are left with extra copies that do not circulate and may need to be weeded due to space concerns. If public librarians have more copies of a title than they need, they can see if the school library media specialist would be interested in the extra books. Create a list of titles of which you have multiple copies, and ask the school library media specialist to share it with the teachers. Even if you own only five or 10 copies of a given title, this still allows a class of students to pick among several titles. One class may read a few different titles, which is a good way to get students to participate in small-group discussions. Offering students a larger selection of materials can help keep them engaged and increase the chances they will actually enjoy a book they are required to read for school.

Another way to exchange books is to supplement classroom collections with public library books on a rotating basis. "In school districts around the nation, administrators have been trying to give kids that easy access to books by investing in classroom libraries. But the classroom libraries have serious limitations. Unlike school libraries, they don't have enough variety or depth to meet the reading interests of many different students. Nor do they provide an organized method of distributing and rotating books."[1] The popularity of teacher collections in the classrooms varies, depending on each teacher's personal resources and preferences, since it is usually the teachers themselves who select and pay for these collections. Recent studies show the importance of surrounding students with a resource-rich environment, and classroom collections can help achieve this goal.

One seventh-grade teacher I booktalked for had an amazing classroom collection of more than 500 paperback books for students to choose from for personal reading. I often brought in a book from the public library, only to find that she already had a copy in the classroom, and she took my lists and purchased additional titles that intrigued her. Her students always had books, and the fact that she was so passionate about books was infectious in itself. Almost every classroom I visited in my local schools (especially English classrooms) contained some kind of in-room collection for students to browse. Not all these collections were varied and current, but students were being exposed to books. Classroom collections play an important role in serving this very real need. So how can school library media specialists and public librarians work to aid teachers in creating or supplementing their classroom collections? What are some potential complications associated with this process?

When the school district my public library served participated in the Reading to Learn conference mentioned in Chapter 5, the participants learned that it is vital for students to be surrounded by books at all times. Not only should the school library media center be well stocked and operated by a professional school library media specialist, but teachers should have classroom collections of 200–500 titles. This allows students to be adequately exposed to books for optimum performance. Simply reading for 15 minutes a day can help increase both test scores and grades, which is why many schools have initiated a Drop Everything and Read program or participate in Sustained Silent Reading. Reading makes kids smarter. Period. Of course, if there are no books for the kids to read, this is impossible. While we wish students could come to the library every day (well, almost every day!), this simply is not practical in many situations, and classroom collections can fill the need in these situations.

Many teachers already have extensive collections in their rooms and freely allow students to use these materials. However, every year new teachers begin their careers, and most have neither the knowledge nor the money to build up a substantial collection in a short amount of time. Others lack the resources or time to create their own collections. Here is where the school library media specialist and the public librarian can work to supplement teachers' efforts.

Create book bins that teachers can check out each semester, either from the school library media center or the public library. These bins can consist of books from the circulating public library collection or donated or withdrawn materials. You can add to the bins after major weeding projects. Go through your collection and select books you have multiple copies of or titles that haven't circulated as well as you expected. At my library, we created a card for each book to let students sign it out of the bin, as in older, nonautomated checkout systems. Of course, how you decide to loan these books depends on whether the books are still part of the public library collection or are discarded materials.

Remember, these collections are not in any way intended to replace the school library media center as the foremost repository for materials in the school. Rather, they are designed to encourage recreational reading.

Book Bin Collections

Here are some basic guidelines to remember when creating a classroom collection:

- Make sure books are in decent shape and not falling apart.
- Set up a system for students to check the books out, especially if they are only on loan from the public library. Outline what will happen if any are lost.
- Try to include a wide variety of genres, including mystery, fantasy, and realistic fiction, as well as assorted nonfiction titles.
- Rotate the bins at least four times a year so that students have access to new materials each quarter.
- Make sure each bin contains at least 60 books so that students have choices.
- At the end of each year (if not more often), check the contents of the bins to ascertain the condition of the books.
- Add to the bins throughout the year, if possible.
- Encourage teachers to read books from the bins and create their own collection.
- Select books based on their appeal to students, not on how they might enhance the curriculum, which is not the purpose of these bins.

Beyond the Printed Book

Libraries are more than just repositories for books. Public libraries often are the first to jump on a new format and show how successful—or not—it may be. (Does anyone remember laserdiscs?) Libraries now loan CD-ROMs, computer games, video games, DVDs, CDs, and audio books in all different formats—and when other formats come along, they too will be offered. Not only should libraries share their books, but they should also share resources in other formats.

Online Resource Sharing

As more resources become available online, you might benefit by working with another library to get joint reduced database pricing from your vendor for both libraries. School library media specialists can also see what databases the public library already offers, determine if their students have access to these, and select additional resources that will supplement what is already available to students elsewhere. This is another a way to share the resources and dollars of the community.

If you would like to try to share a database contract with another library, first determine who has the purchasing power. A school library media specialist or youth services librarian may not have the final say in what databases are purchased for their libraries. If this is the case, find out who *can* make these decisions. Sit down to talk about the databases you feel would benefit students. Give them numbers. For instance, if you are in a school library serving 1,000 students, estimate how often each student might access the database for assigned research projects over the school year. Numbers talk to those with the power to make these decisions.

When signing a joint contract, each library might contribute a percentage of the cost, based on expected usage. Approach the vendor with numbers and statistics to back up your claim that your clientele overlap to help justify your request for reduced joint pricing. Since there will be overlap, it seems crazy for a school district and a public library both to pay for the same database.

Of course many libraries are in situations in which their school districts do not perfectly overlap their boundaries. In larger suburban areas, the public library district might serve some of the students in many schools, but not all of the students in any one school. What about students who live in unincorporated areas not served by public library districts and whose parents who will not pay for a library card? Do you penalize these students by disallowing them access to the databases they need for school research? In many such cases, school districts end up simply purchasing their own online subscriptions. It may not be feasible for the school and the public library to get a joint contract, but do look into the possibility. With your discount you may have some leftover money to spend on additional, more specialized databases.

If you have negotiated a contract with a vendor, be aware of its terms and limitations. School library media specialists need to be cognizant of these when deciding to use public library databases for their students. Each school and public library district throughout the country operates slightly differently. In some places, the county negotiates with vendors to get residents countywide access. In state-negotiated contracts, the whole state has access. Many public libraries limit database access to registered users by requiring a library card number. This is another reason to have the public librarians visit the schools to register students for cards. Stress the potential hits to public library databases, which will also help justify subscription renewals. Students who have library cards can use public library databases at school and at home, rather than only at the public library, where there might not be enough computers to accommodate all the students. With some time and patience, both libraries can come out on top in terms of usage, as well as in extending funding.

DVDs, CD-ROMs, and Other Nonprint Formats

Many public libraries subscribe to ebooks online and purchase Playaways (audiobooks on small battery-run players), DVDs, CDs, and computer games. Sharing nonprint items offers libraries another way to supplement the curriculum while increasing circulation statistics.

As with any resource sharing, first determine the need. As a school library media specialist with very limited funds, you may be at a loss when a teacher asks for the latest documentary about sharks but your collection's most recent video dates back to the mid-1990s. While the public library may carry some documentaries on sharks, these might also be outdated; many public libraries focus more heavily on popular materials in nonprint formats. Of course, ILL is always an option, but it can take time—and we all know teachers who mention they need something the day before they would like to use it. Here is where communicating curricular needs to the public library can be very valuable.

If a school library media specialist can show that teachers are likely to check out a public library DVD on, say, sharks at least three times per year because it supplements the curriculum, the public library will find purchasing such a product much more attractive. Public librarians can consult with school librarians to find out if there are particular curriculum areas in which nontraditional formats would be useful. Supporting the schools in this manner is productive; however, follow-up is crucial to ensure that school library media specialists then know what is available from the public library.

Consider working together to organize a series of documentary showings at the public library, using the library's video collection, designed to highlight certain areas of the curriculum. Each year, the school library media specialist could work with teachers to determine extra material that students would benefit from but that they might not have time to view in the classroom. Encourage teachers to offer extra credit to students who attend showings of this material at the public library. This arrangement offers students the opportunity to expand their knowledge without requiring teachers to give up valuable classroom time; it offers an opportunity for the school library media specialist to work in conjunction with the public librarian; and it offers an easy way for the public library to present a program that showcases part of its collection—and that is guaranteed to be well-attended!

Of course, public libraries need to be aware of copyright laws when showing DVDs and videos in public. While schools are allowed to show videos to classes if the material is aligned with their curriculum, public libraries need to secure performance rights. Try to purchase materials with public performance rights included in the price, especially if you are likely to use them in programming. Otherwise, you will need to secure the right to show the material before proceeding with your program. Secure rights through clearinghouses such as Movie Licensing USA (www.movlic.com) and the Motion Picture Licensing Company (www.mplc.com).

Themes for video-based programs might include the Holocaust, Native Americans, the Civil War, the Vietnam War, colonialism, explorers, the Civil Rights movement, the Revolutionary War, or any number of science-related programs, from global warming to oceans to dinosaurs. See what topics support the curriculum in your own schools. And don't miss this opportunity to display related materials for students to check out after the show!

On the Road Again

One idea for bringing the public library to the school is via a book-mobile. My former library had debated adding a third library to our district, but we realized that a referendum to support this move was unlikely to pass. We then turned to the idea of adding a bookmobile, which could take materials into underserved areas of the community. The bookmobile also began to visit schools to help supplement their collections, give students access to a wider selection of popular materials, and bring requested books to the school library media specialists.

At first, I was skeptical. After all, I was already visiting hundreds of students at the middle schools each month, while a children's department staff member visited the elementary schools. How would students get from their classrooms to the bookmobile? What about in the winter, when they would need coats? Would teachers bring their own students, or would the school library media specialists be responsible? What if students didn't have a library card? So many questions and potential problems kept cropping up in my mind.

When the bookmobile was launched, most of the problems I had anticipated seemed to disappear. The schools were *thrilled* to have this service. Teachers, school library media specialists, and principals alike embraced the bookmobile. Yes, students did need a library card to make use of its services, but this created a push to get students registered—helping our statistics in the process. The school library media specialists were instrumental in this effort, and I worked with middle school librarians and the bookmobile staff to get cards to students in a timely fashion. When I spent time on the bookmobile, I was delighted to be able to do intensive reader's advisory with students I knew and recognized from my booktalking visits. The bookmobile stocked the books I talked to the students about, so I had many popular titles at my fingertips. It was invigorating to see students outside of their classroom and watch their selection processes up close and personal in this small space. In the public library, I was removed from the teens' actual decision-making process unless I approached them or they requested my assistance. Problems with the bookmobile did arise, but most were overcome by cooperation between the school library media specialists and the bookmobile staff, and sometimes myself as intermediary. We achieved our goal of serving the youth and expanding their access to resources and materials. And as for winter—hey, kids can run fast when it's cold!

Only a fraction of public library districts currently operate a bookmobile. Rural districts may use this service to visit small towns in their area, and larger systems may use a bookmobile if they do not have many branches or their population is less mobile. The cost of this service can in many cases be prohibitive. However, if you have a bookmobile in your area, see if it is possible for it to make visits to the schools. Make the time to find out what services are offered, and see how these can be utilized to bring more assets to the clientele you serve.

Keeping It Real

As always, when contemplating sharing resources, be realistic. If your administrator or principal refuses to share funds with other agencies, it will be difficult for you to suggest that your public library use funds to create classroom sets for school use, or that your school jointly invest in an online database with the public library. If your ability to support online databases is compromised due to limited technology, sharing database subscriptions may not benefit your library. Working around limitations and seeing the possibilities are part of what we as librarians do every day; sometimes we just need another librarian to bounce ideas and "what if's" off of. Sharing makes the impossible seem possible.

Endnote

1. Debra Gniewek, "The Rotating Library," *School Library Journal* 46:8 (2000): 35.

Chapter 8

Visits

*"Why did I volunteer to give a booktalk to 300 freshmen?"
I wondered nervously, as I began driving to the high
school. "They're going to yawn in my face, turn my book-
marks into paper airplanes, start working on homework,
put their head down on the desks."… As I pulled up to the
school, I couldn't help thinking: "What am I doing here?"*
—Jennifer Bromann[1]

The most invigorating, engaging, informative, time-consuming,
and rewarding interactions you will have with another library are
visits—whether a public librarian visits the school or a school
librarian brings students to the public library. These visits give
librarians a chance to see the other "world" and to gain a greater
understanding of how their counterparts function. Visits also allow
public library staff to see students in a different manner than they
are typically used to and let teachers and students connect with a
public librarian outside the boundaries of the public library building. Visits can be wildly successful—or disastrous. Careful planning, as well as acknowledging your own strengths and
weaknesses, will help you decide if you should invest your time
and energy into visits.

School Visits

Over the years I developed many personal relationships with
teachers and school library media specialists, largely by booktalking at the middle schools in my district. It started gradually and
then took on a life of its own. I still visit the home of one retired

teacher and keep in regular contact with teachers and library media specialists at the schools, even though I no longer work at the public library. These relationships were nurtured through my time in the classrooms, during school visits to the public library, and through my role as liaison between the schools and the public library. They will continue to be invaluable as I begin my new career as a school library media specialist. However, as with all relationships, not every day went perfectly when we were working together. Hindsight is always 20/20. Acknowledging mistakes and learning from them helps mend fences and maintain relationships, both with the people you work with and those you are trying to serve.

Booktalks

Booktalks are near and dear to my heart and always will be. Most simply, a booktalk is a presentation in which you share information about a book to entice students to want to read it. A booktalk for an individual title can range from 30 seconds to five minutes, depending on the presenter's preferences. The talks typically involve providing details about the book in a way that captivates the students, inspiring them to check the book out and read it.

When I first ventured into the classroom, I had been at my job for just a few months and had given only practice booktalks in library school. Standing up in front of a group of library students and running through a mock booktalk differs greatly from booktalking to 30 middle school students, in which case you know that the teacher is watching you and deciding if you will be allowed a repeat performance. That first time, I just introduced myself, booktalked three books, and promoted a library program. I read off of note cards and only spent 15 minutes in the classroom. Still, this gave me my first taste of booktalking. It also gave me a chance to chat with the school library media specialist, which began a great working relationship that lasted until she retired seven years later. Building rapport with students and teachers takes time and a *lot* of effort. It pays to start small, as this allows you to hone your craft and quickly change your strategies if they are not working. Not everyone is cut out to be a booktalker, and there is no shame in this. We all have strengths and weaknesses; our ability to focus on our strengths while understanding our weaknesses helps us to fulfill our duties to the youth we serve.

That being said, let's say you are ready to try a booktalk—or 10! Public librarians will need the assistance of their school library media specialist in everything from getting teachers' schedules to determining students' reading abilities. School library media specialists who love giving booktalks often find they lack the time to prepare and present as many as they would like. Here is the perfect opportunity to reach out to the public librarian and invite her to contribute. For example, perhaps a teacher wants each student to read a historical novel set during the Civil War, but the school's collection can't support that assignment. This is an ideal time to call in the public library and its expanded resources, allowing it to promote its collection while supplementing your own. So, where do you begin?

Know Thyself

Booktalking can be frightening at first, especially if you are not used to working with groups of students. School library media specialists have an advantage over their public library counterparts here since they present to classes every day. Still, booktalking differs from giving a database demonstration or a presentation on correctly citing sources. Let the storyteller in you come out, using voices, sound, movement—not a whole lot is off limits in a booktalk! After all, you are giving a performance, which hopefully will translate into getting a student interested in a book.

For more details on how to conduct a booktalk, check out titles such as *Booktalking That Works,* by Jennifer Bromann; *Booktalking Authentic Multicultural Literature: Fiction, History, and Memoirs for Teens,* by Sherry York; and *Gotcha!: Nonfiction Booktalks to Get Kids Excited About Reading,* by Kathleen Baxter and Marcia Agness Kochel.

Keep in mind, though, that what you read in a book and what works with your personality and presentation style might differ. Your booktalks should reflect your own personality, for only then will you be comfortable executing them class after class, day after day. For some people, booktalking will never be fun, or even comfortable—but with the right attitude, some preparation, and a huge amount of patience, your time spent in the classroom can be rewarding. Perhaps you will discover, as I did, that your true passion is working with students.

Getting There

You have decided to begin presenting booktalks. Now, as a public librarian, you need to get *into* the schools! Here is where all that time you have spent communicating with school library media specialists will pay off in spades. Your goal all along may have been to booktalk your collection and connect with the students in a whole different setting, but you need to first establish a basic level of trust with your counterpart.

Contact your school library media specialists to see if they would be interested in having you do a booktalk related to a yearly project at the school, say on books about the Underground Railroad. This topical approach is especially helpful in the secondary grades. At the elementary level, you can offer an abridged storytime with books and perhaps a puppet. Ask how you can add to the program the school library media specialist already has in place, rather than taking it over or creating a competing program. Remember, booktalking is part of most school library media specialists' duties, especially in the younger grades. If a teacher contacts you and requests a booktalk, mention this to the school library media specialist—the teacher may have no idea that the school librarian offers booktalks as well. Avoid stepping on your colleagues' toes, and communicate openly with your counterpart in order to build trust.

Once you have arranged to bring your booktalks to the school, determine which teachers and grade level(s) you will present to, what topic(s) you will cover, and how much time will be allocated for you in the classroom or school library media center. Booktalks should optimally occur in the classroom, both to maximize the available time and to allow the school library media center to continue its regularly scheduled activities. It is easier for you to walk from room to room with your bag of books than for groups of students to move into the school library, which takes time away from hearing about books and gives them time to get excited—in a *bad* way! In the classroom, presumably they are already in their seats and understand the rules of their class. Here are some issues to consider:

- Make sure teachers know that you expect them to stay in the room while you are booktalking. Most teachers view you as a guest speaker and will treat you as such; however, especially your first time, make it clear you are visiting and not there to sub.

- Get a copy of the bell schedule ahead of time; this is crucial in a middle, junior, or high school setting.

- Establish the time you have for your presentation. Your initial presentation might last just 20 minutes, but once you have confidence, you might want to try to cover the entire period.

- Ask for a school map. You might have only a few minutes to get from class to class, so having a map (with teachers' names clearly marked) will help.

- Find out if and when you will have time for lunch. You might forget to schedule yourself a break! If you can, eat with the school library media specialist or in the school library to get a taste of the environment and help foster your relationship. Eating with the school library media specialist in the teacher's lounge is a good way to make contacts and inform teachers of your presence.

- Don't spread yourself too thin. It can be easy to get excited and offer booktalks to everyone who asks. If you have more than six full periods scheduled in one day, seriously consider a second visit. I once did seven full periods—never again! Booktalking in the classroom gives you a whole new respect for teachers.
- Bring water, a snack, and something to read, in case you have a moment of down time.

Scheduling might be your biggest challenge. The school library media specialist can help by trying to keep you in one part of the building in the morning and another part in the afternoon, but you are at the mercy of an established timetable. Remember to try to give yourself time between booktalks, even if it's just five minutes.

So Many Books ... So Little Time

One of your most daunting tasks is selecting your titles. For example, I was once asked to booktalk books on World War I. "No problem," I thought. I hadn't read any on that topic, but surely I could find some and read them quickly. Well, I promptly discovered that we owned very few fiction titles covering that time period. Whoops. I guess I should have checked the catalog before making promises. I supplemented my talk with nonfiction titles—which actually is a good approach, since many readers prefer nonfiction. Still, this experience taught me a lesson: Check before committing. Your choices on a specific topic are limited by your collection. This goes double for school library media specialists, especially if this is a subject that is new to the curriculum or one that a teacher has chosen to delve into more deeply than before. This is a perfect time to invite a public librarian to come in or to request titles from the public library that you can booktalk yourself. This approach also gives you an opportunity to "preview" titles you might want to add to your collection and to gauge how popular the material might be in your school.

In many cases, though, you will face the opposite problem: too many books, too little time, too many choices. When you booktalk, it is important to bring in books you enjoy, but also books students can connect with. Don't bring out your favorite Jane Austen title, no matter how strongly you feel it retains its relevance. Teens who want Jane Austen will find her, and you will only lose credibility by showing you are out of touch with the students. As a librarian who works with youth, you already have an idea of what students like reading. Your job as a booktalker is to bring to their attention other books that they might also enjoy but don't yet know about. Students always asked me why I didn't booktalk the *Harry Potter* books, and I responded by asking anyone who hadn't heard of *Harry Potter* to raise their hands. Of course, no hands would go up. I didn't booktalk *Harry Potter* because students already knew about *Harry Potter*; my job was to tell them about books they didn't know about.

Gauging your books to the reading ability of the class(es) you visit is important as well. I received many requests for booktalks on high-interest/low-reading-level books; requests for these titles on lists and in libraries show this is a growing need. These sorts of titles are harder to find than you might think, because they need to appeal to the students' age group, not just fit their reading level. Always try to bring at least one book that would engage a student with lower reading abilities. In this same vein, keep in mind how many of the main characters in each book are boys. Girls don't care, but boys do, so be cognizant of this. Try to include a variety of ethnic and socioeconomic backgrounds in your choices—this may not work for every topic, but make a conscious effort to bring a wide variety to your booktalks over time.

Take the time to create an annotated list of all the books you present. Specify the school and grade, the date of the booktalk, and its topic or theme. Give a copy to each teacher you visit (or who visits your school library) to save students from having to write down titles during your presentation (and thus creating a distraction) and to provide a reference for teachers. Also give the list to the school library media specialist so that she can order copies of the titles or set aside the books in the school library and alert teachers. Keep a binder of these booktalk lists at the public library as well, in the space where the majority of the books discussed are located. These lists become invaluable over time as a ready resource for other staff members, a reader's advisory resource for those unfamiliar with children's and young adult books, and a reference for you to look up what titles you have already booktalked.

They Aren't Listening to Me

Classroom management is no laughing matter, as teachers and school library media specialists can attest. Basic classroom management techniques always apply, regardless of the purpose of your visit. Public librarians should not be alone in the classroom or school library with the students. The teacher is your first line of defense during presentations; students will be much more respectful of you and what you have to share if their teacher is present. Remember that the mood of a class can change in an instant, and you have to be ready to react quickly to keep students focused. Here are some tips to keep in mind when presenting to students:

- Be prepared! No one likes to see someone fumble through his bag, realize his notes are out of order, or find that his PowerPoint presentation isn't compatible with the school's system. Practice your presentation before you go to the school so that you can concentrate on the students and their reactions rather than on what you are going to say next.

- Assess the students. In the mornings, older students tend to be less responsive—simply because they are tired! I was told that Neal Shusterman will not even see eighth-grade students during first period on his author visits; he obviously knows they aren't awake at that time. Try not to be discouraged if your jokes fall flat early in the day; they will probably get laughs later.

- Engage the students by building in ways to interact with them. This keeps you aware of their behavior and lets them know you are watching. Plus, if you keep them occupied and stimulated, they won't have as many reasons to pass notes to each other. A simple way to interact is to ask questions periodically.

- Walk around the room. Simply moving about forces students to focus their attention on you. If you have a student—or several students—who are ignoring you, bring them into the presentation by asking them point-blank questions. Get names, if you can. One teacher always gave me her seating chart, and I found it amazing how quickly a student would quiet down once I mentioned his name a few times.

- Enjoy yourself with the students, and let them see your enjoyment. Allow yourself to get a bit personal with the students, and them with you.

Know when you are in over your head in classroom management, and be open about your concerns. If a class gets out of hand, even with the teacher or school librarian in the room (this does happen), be honest with the school about this afterwards. Explain that you had some issues maintaining students' interest and that you are not sure if the students would benefit from another talk since most did not seem focused during your visit. If you feel up to it, give the class another try. If it still doesn't work, it's time to drop this teacher or this presentation from your rotation for the year. If you really want to see the class(es), limit your time and offer abbreviated presentations.

The key to any presentation at the school is deciding whether you enjoy the process. If you dread presenting, or if you feel defeated after a day at the school, it might be best to acknowledge that these visits are not for you. You may be able to ask another staff member to provide booktalks or instructional services to students, while you concentrate on other productive ways to serve your population.

Instruction Time

In general, public libraries tend to have more resources available and more funds to expend than do school libraries. In particular, public libraries usually subscribe to more online databases. As mentioned in Chapter 7, sharing these resources might be in your best interest. Even if the databases are available only through the public library, students can access them there or remotely with a public library card. Providing instruction to the schools on how to use public library resources benefits students and allows teachers to see what materials can be used to supplement the curriculum.

School library media specialists may not be familiar with the database offerings at the public library and may not have time to research the ins and outs of each product. Invite a public librarian in to give a presentation on using these databases. School librarians typically know what teachers are interested in helping students achieve, so when you contact the public librarian, give him an idea of what type of information is being sought so that he can identify the most suitable databases. Discuss how long the presentation will take, and lay out what you and the teachers are anticipating the students to learn. Make your expectations for the instruction clear.

When planning for a public librarian's visit, clearly outline the technology setup at the school. Will the public librarian need to bring his own laptop? Will he need to access the school's network? Is the hardware compatible? Will you be able to establish an Internet connection? How will the demonstration be conducted? Will students work on their own computers in a lab, or will the presentation simply be projected onto a screen? Both librarians need to be clear on the physical setup and the hardware and software available for this type of demonstration.

School librarians give informational presentations and instruction on a daily basis. Public librarians should make sure to supplement, rather than duplicate, existing instruction, whether on databases or other topics. Ask what your school librarian is interested in having you present. Possible programs include:

- An overview of the public library's services and upcoming programs

- How to search the public library's online catalog, and where items are located in the building

- How to use ILL to get materials through the public library, with a discussion of the procedures and rules and what types of materials are obtainable

- An overview of specialized database(s) that contain information relevant to specific research projects or papers

- Internet search strategies, including tips on critically evaluating websites for accuracy and authenticity

Simply giving school library media specialists a list of possible programs may spark ideas for topics they would like to see covered but lack the time to provide themselves. You can also offer to present collaboratively with the school library media specialist. Planning a joint presentation provides a wonderful opportunity for you to work together and grow your relationship. Joint presentations take more time to put together but will give you more credibility with the students and offer valuable experience working collaboratively outside of your library.

School visits can be very productive for both librarians, as well as for the students. You create new links in your relationship and more possibilities for long-term association. Initial visits may require a tremendous amount of planning and background work, but once a procedure has been established, visits can become routine. Change things up if they don't work for you, and keep the lines of communication open.

Public Library Visits

School library media specialists can relate to this scenario: A teacher comes into your library and starts grumbling about how you have no resources on a subject her students are studying while the public library has so many—and why is that, by the way? Possibly because your library is designed to serve 1,500 students and the public library serves more than 40,000 residents? Or possibly because your funding has been cut for the fourth year in a row, and you have been reduced to purchasing books with book fair money and PTA funds? There will come a time when a teacher presents you with a topic or unit of study, and you know you will not be able to adequately meet her needs. This problem can often be remedied by supplementing your collection with books from the public library. However, if your public library does not loan out batches of books as part of its service to the schools or will not allow certain materials to be taken out of the library, it might be time to consider a field trip to the public library.

Planning a Trip

Planning a student outing to the public library is no easy feat. It is more convenient for one public librarian to come to a school than for hundreds of students to go to the public library during a school day—and for public library staff to deal with the havoc these visits can create. Over the years, I learned how to minimize the stress these visits created yet still give students and teachers the service they needed.

A simple trip to the public library brings a whole host of responsibilities for school librarians. Even if students can walk there, each must still have parental permission to be off school grounds. What happens when a student doesn't bring back the requisite paperwork, and is forced to stay behind? Who will watch him? If the library is located farther away, you must arrange for a bus, find the money to pay for the trip, and factor in the time taken away from other classes. Of course, most teachers are aware of these stumbling blocks, and they presumably have decided that the problems are offset by the benefits: the resources their students can access in the public library that the school cannot currently provide.

The first step in planning any visit is to establish a time frame. Call your contact at the public library. Discuss what the teacher wants to have happen (e.g., students will locate a historical novel, use online databases to research a paper, check out books) and the amount of time available. To ensure that the date(s) discussed do not conflict with other library events, public librarians should check with their circulation, adult services, and youth services departments and any other important areas where the students might need assistance during their visit or where their presence might impact work flow or other programs. For example, if the school wants to visit on a day when the youth services department already has three storytimes scheduled, this would be less than ideal. Of course, you can make only so many accommodations before you start to go crazy, but try to minimize the strain a visit will put on the library staff.

Set up one spot as a staging area, especially if large groups of students will be coming and going throughout the day. This lets the public librarian in charge of the visit give instructions, pass out materials, and remind students of their expected conduct in the library, which will keep disruption to a minimum for regular library patrons. Students can leave their books and papers here and can use this room to work in groups if necessary. Identify at least one additional public library staff member to work with the students and teacher(s) and to troubleshoot any issues and serve as the go-between for students and the public library staff.

Allow enough time for the prescribed activities, and understand the technological limitations of your facility. For instance, if the teacher wants the students to understand, access, and retrieve information from the public library's databases, and you only have four terminals available for student use, you might find it difficult to conduct an adequate demonstration. If your library has a computer lab, consider holding such a demonstration in the lab.

Preparing for a Visit

Public librarians can take steps to make any school visit as productive as possible:

- Get a copy of the assignment ahead of time. Pull relevant materials before students arrive.
- Set up a staging area, such as a large meeting room, where you can give directions, rules, and explanations and answer any questions before turning students loose. This area also gives visiting students a home base to return to once they have located their resources and allows you to work with smaller groups if you need to provide instruction.
- Email a reminder to library staff the day before the visit is scheduled. Make sure you address any concerns they have raised.
- Open up one copy machine for free copies, in case a student forgets or runs out of money.
- Follow up with other staff members and departments after the visit. Ask if they experienced any problems, and ask for suggestions on how to improve the next visit.

School library media specialists can also help ensure productive visits:

- Contact the public librarian you are working with and ask about any specific requirements for the visit.
- Check with teacher(s) to make sure permission slips have been sent home and transportation is available.
- Establish a working schedule with the teacher(s) and the public library.
- Discuss the assignment or teachers' expectations with the public librarian ahead of time.
- Ensure that each student has a library card prior to the visit.
- Check in after the visit to see how it went and if anything should be changed for the next time.

If time is limited, pull materials ahead of time and create hand-outs for students. I had yearly visits from three classes in which the students had to do extensive research papers on a country they had selected. Their teacher always supplied me with a list of the countries a few days ahead of time so that I could pull books and photocopy information from various sources for the students. The limited time for their visit did not allow the students to find these materials themselves. We also allowed students to make free photocopies, so they did not have to worry about bringing in money. This system allowed me to assist students in finding the information they needed for their papers and relieved the rest of the staff of any added burdens the visit might otherwise have placed on them.

Think of anything that might go wrong, and then have a contingency plan in place. For example, your copiers are broken, the circulation system goes down, the Internet connection isn't working … in other words, Murphy's Law. If the worst does happen, the trip may even have to be postponed. Discuss what will happen in the event of a cancellation; if possible, work a "rain date" into the permission slips and the public library's calendar.

Are They Gone Yet?

Waving to the last sixth grader running out of the public library door, you put your hand to your pounding head and think, Thank goodness that visit is over! Even the most productive and well-run visit can be exhausting. A school library media specialist's role might be very involved, or minor, depending on your teachers and the goal of the visit. A public librarian's role will probably be extensive, including setting up the visit, preparing for the visit, and being present on the day of the visit. Some visits may be pleasant, even calm; others may seem like a three-ring circus. Taking the steps outlined in the preceding section will help alleviate some of the inherent stresses.

The No. 1 reason student trips are dreaded by public library staff is the issue of student behavior in the library. Most public libraries have faced behavior problems with students after school (see

Chapter 4), which can contribute to these concerns. However, class visits differ from after-school situations: You have a teacher present and can bring any undesirable behavior to her attention.

Be very frank with teachers and school library media specialists who ask about a visit to the public library. Establish consequences for inappropriate student behavior. Most often, misbehaving students must stay with the teacher, but this means she is then less free to assist the other students. The best way to impress upon students what you expect from them in the way of conduct is simply to tell them. Be very clear in laying out the public library's expectations. Remind them that this is still school and that they are at the library for a specific reason. Make sure students understand that other patrons are using the library at the same time and that they need to be courteous. The older the students, the less you have to harp on this, but a gentle prompt is never amiss.

Reflecting

As a school library media specialist, your role in visits may be limited to the planning stages. As a public librarian, you may arrange only a few class visits per year to the library and a few librarian visits to the school, or you might devote the majority of your time to these visits. Whatever your level of involvement, visits provide amazing opportunities for growth. Building on your relationship in this way will strengthen the bonds between your libraries and enable you to continue to develop your collaborative relationship.

Endnote

1. Jennifer Bromann, "The Toughest Audience on Earth," *School Library Journal* 45:10 (1999): 60–63.

Chapter 9

Garnering Support

Sometimes we have a great idea for a partnership, cooperative project, or collaboration. We present it to our supervisor or administrator, who gasps in irritation, "How much time do you need away from the public service desk?" or, "What is wrong with the collection in the school library? Are you saying we don't give you enough money?" Finding the time, support, and funding to collaborate can be tricky. We wish for more time in our day (and money in our budget) just to complete our regularly assigned tasks. Still, collaboration is an ingrained part of who we are as librarians, and creating new, innovative ways to serve our populations is a high priority for us.

Inspiring others with the same passion and perspective is not always easy. Yet without the active, if not joyous, support of your supervisor(s), little can be accomplished. Navigating between the demands of a less-than-supportive supervisor and the needs of your population can be difficult at times—and downright frustrating at others. Understanding the motivation behind your supervisor's behavior can help you find the hidden key(s) to unlocking support for your cause. Recognize that a supportive supervisor is important, and find ways to show her how much her backing means to a productive library environment. This can go a long way toward furthering many collaborative plans.

Often a project may require financial backing. One way to garner support for joint projects with another library is to look outside your own institutions for funding for your partnership. Libraries' funds are inherently limited, and grants can supplement what you are able to do with your own resources.

Getting Grants

When facing a monetary shortfall for any joint project, consider the possibility of applying for a grant. Since the grant application process tends to be stressful, though, it's not advisable to start a relationship off by working on a grant; as always, take time to lay the foundation for your partnership before embarking on more ambitious projects. The hardest part of getting a grant is locating the right opportunity for your project. However, it may encourage you to know that people are frequently awarded grants because there were so few applicants!

Knowing where to look for grants is as important as writing a winning grant proposal. Start locally; ask around. Your colleagues might be a valuable resource. Ask a librarian who always seems to be getting grants where she looks for possible funding sources. Check with your local library systems and your state library association. Nationally, investigate Grants.gov (www.grants.gov), a keyword-searchable site that collocates thousands of grants offered by government agencies. Another fabulous site for school and public libraries is Follett's Grants and Funding page (www.titlewave.com/intro/grants.html). This site lists grants for areas such as after-school program funding, PTOs, and summer programs and includes funding opportunities from places that you might never think of, such as the Dollar Store. Be sure also to consult the Library Grants blog (librarygrants.blogspot.com), and check out its authors' book, *Grants for Libraries* (Neal-Schuman, 2006), for useful advice on the process.

Typically, funders want to see grant recipients work collaboratively or cooperatively with other community organizations. Many like to see matching funds or a commitment to continuing the project after the grant ends. Here is where your relationship with the other library comes into play; it will be easier to get grants for collaborative projects than to go it alone. It also is easier to work with someone you have already established a connection with than to go out and beat on doors.

The Lay of the Land

You usually can fairly quickly assess how receptive your supervisor is to your working with another library; a feel for the climate of your institution will give you further insight into the likelihood of long-term success. Still, you may be shocked to be turned down when you propose visiting the school to give a booktalk or inviting a public librarian in to demonstrate databases. A previously congenial supervisor may see problems where you do not and frustrate your ability to connect in a meaningful way. Keep in mind that your supervisor might not be used to working directly with the population you serve (as is the case, for example, when a young adult librarian needs permission from a supervisor in the adult services department) or might not see why this crossover service is necessary (as is the case when a principal wants to keep it in the school). Understanding your supervisor's position and biases will help you define the challenges you face in working with the other library.

Testing the Water

You have decided you want to work with another library but aren't sure how this will be perceived or received by your supervisor. At the outset, you aren't likely to need a five-page proposal on the pros and cons of your project. Rather, start with something you know will catch your supervisor's eye in a positive way and will reflect well on your library or school. If you sense he may have issues with your partnership, begin to pave the way by collecting articles that discuss the benefits of libraries, working together and pooling their resources. Shirley Fitzgibbons has done extensive work on the importance of working in concert, and you can find a number of other resources in the Recommended Reading section at the end of this book. Give your supervisor a copy of a relevant article, with a note attached suggesting that you chat about its ideas. Your supervisor may be inspired to revisit his views on the subject or, in a best-case scenario, may even contribute ideas on how you could collaborate.

Your ultimate goal also determines the way in which you gain support for your projects and the amount of support you will need. Are you interested in having the local public librarian present information about her summer reading program at an assembly? To justify pulling students out of class, you need to convince your principal of the importance of reading over the summer. Do you want to give booktalks every year to eighth graders studying the Holocaust? You need your supervisor to schedule sufficient off-desk time for you to visit the school. Are you hoping to launch a yearlong collaborative project involving a grant, an author visit, and ongoing book discussion groups? Break down what you want to do into smaller parts if you foresee trouble getting approval from the powers that be. This strategy lets you evaluate each component for possible problems and look at the issues from the other person's perspective. For example, does your principal hate large assemblies because the students get crazy and the teachers use this time to chat in the back of the gym? Scale back your plans, and hold the summer reading presentations in the school library media center or propose a smaller, more manageable assembly for each grade. Does your supervisor need coverage on a service desk? See if you can switch shifts with a coworker, and explain the potential benefits of your project in terms of increased circulation. Create a proposal that preemptively deals with any objection(s) your supervisor may have. This will reassure him that you understand how the venture could be construed as an imposition but will also help convince him that in the long run it will benefit both parties involved.

If your supervisor has previously reacted negatively to the idea of collaboration or partnering, begin keeping statistics. Start with a period of six months, which is long enough to show measurable results from many ventures. In a school setting, some of your power will come from test scores. Under the No Child Left Behind Act, many good schools are struggling to make adequate yearly progress. Suggest that allowing students access to a wider variety of resources—more than can be provided with the funds from the school—will increase scores; offer to track students' progress. This proposal might give you more credence with your principal. Never forget the power of the dollar—as in any dollar *not* being spent out of the school coffers. One K–12 librarian in Caldwell, Ohio, brings this point home, saying: "As to administration being sold on the collaboration: It was not difficult because it was a way to benefit students without using funding dollars. Most administrators can be persuaded when the request doesn't include currency."

The same goes for a public librarian who, for instance, wants to booktalk in the schools. Keep track of how many children come up to the desk and request a specific title over a six-month period. Absent booktalks, this number will probably be minimal (unless you include the *Harry Potter* series!). Argue that you want to see whether booktalks make a difference in this number and in your circulation statistics; this might attract your supervisor's notice. Do a trial series of booktalks, and the results may give you more ammunition for creating an ongoing program.

Moving to Motivation

Sometimes you just seem to hit a brick wall—not for lack of trying on your part, but due to a supervisor's biases. She may have a personal reason for not wanting to support the other library or may truly feel that this sort of collaboration pulls funds and time away from your own institution. Have an honest talk with her and see if you can get to the root of the issue. For instance, a public librarian might encounter comments like:

- "Have you seen how much tax money goes to the schools? They need to fund their own libraries better."

- "You were hired to work at this library, not at the school library. We pay your salary; they don't."

- "Why should we help them? They have nothing to do with what we do."

These statements may seem harsh, but the sentiment in some cases is very real. This kind of reaction can be frustrating and hard to understand—especially if your supervisor is normally quite supportive.

Addressing biases can be difficult. If your supervisor responds to the idea of collaboration with one of these statements, begin with a proposal that *unequivocally* benefits your library: summer reading, library card sign-ups, or program promotion. Once some of these "baby steps" have gone well, you may see a gradual change of opinion. (To bolster your case, keep statistics! For example: how many students signed up for summer reading from X school, where the program was promoted, versus how many from Y school, where it was not.) Sometimes, a supervisor's negative comments might be brought on by stress. Has funding gone down? Have personnel changes resulted in a lack of staff? Has something upsetting happened in your supervisor's personal life? If you suspect these comments stem from stress, rather than long-standing belief, wait a few months and present your idea again with a slightly different twist. Time can work wonders.

Those working in school library media centers face a different set of issues when dealing with their administration. Most principals gladly welcome any support from the public library. As many school library media specialists can attest, the school library can often feel like its own little island in the school, and this position can be both a blessing and a curse—in the case of collaboration with another institution, it's often a blessing. You can most likely invite a public librarian in with little fuss or controversy. You might, however, have the dubious distinction of working in a school where the principal does have some issues with sharing resources or having public librarians come into the school. You may hear comments like:

- "If the public library can come here, why do we need you?"

- "What if this gets back to the school board, and they think we aren't funding the school library? How will that make me look?"

- "We don't need any outside support. You can do it all."

If you have ever heard one of these remarks, you probably wanted to head for the hills! Still, it pays to realize that these are insecurities being voiced, and they don't necessarily reflect on your performance as a school library media specialist.

Carefully review what has been said and try to uncover the real reason you have been denied support. Then, get some of the teachers on your side. Work out a concrete reason for why the public library's assistance is being sought. Show the principal how working together will benefit students and staff and help keep costs down. If nothing else works, playing the money card should!

Encouraging and Rewarding Support

Your supervisor very likely does—or will—see the advantages and positive aspects of working with the other library. Most people who work for and with youth understand that it takes many people to meet their needs. When you have a supportive supervisor, take the time to keep him informed. Keep a record of what you do with the other library. Keep track of statistics, and document positive feedback, such as cards you receive from teachers and students and any other positive remarks regarding your partnership. Continuing to promote the collaboration to your supervisor is just as important as getting it established in the first place.

In a school setting, keep your principal informed about your partnerships and collaborations with the public library. Alert your principal when the public librarian comes for a visit. (You might keep him posted on a monthly basis if she visits quite often.)

Knowing the Benefits

An interview with Helen Poyer, associate director of Branch Services, Cobb County Public Library System, Marietta, Georgia.

Q: How important is it in your mind to work with public school districts—speaking as an administrator?
A: I think it is extremely important to develop a working relationship with public school districts. Schools and libraries are institutions that share very similar missions and goals. We both are committed to developing lifelong learners. We both promote literacy and the importance and rewards of reading. An important mission of educators and librarians is to nurture the educational development of young people in our communities. In the process, we strive to develop a community of learners who will one day become contributors to our diverse and changing society.

As the cost of operating and maintaining our public institutions increases and our economy slows, the need for schools and libraries to work together becomes even greater. With funding always being a challenge for public institutions, the need to better coordinate and leverage scarce resources to achieve the fundamental goal of maintaining the educational foundation for our young people becomes of even greater importance. School media centers strive to provide the up-to-date library materials needed for research and needed to support the curriculum units. The public library is able to provide fiction and nonfiction titles for leisure reading as well as for school projects. Working together, schools and libraries can better meet the reading needs of a more diverse student population and community.

Q: What areas of overlap do you perceive between school and public libraries?

A: There could be an overlap in collection development. Popular fiction and nonfiction authors and titles could be found in both settings; however, the public library that develops collections for leisure reading as well as educational would have multiple copies of those popular authors and titles. The school media center would focus more on those titles that would support the implementation of the curriculum and more likely not have multiple copies.

Q: What are some of the indicators you would like to have to support, or to justify if needed, involvement with the schools?

A: Statistics are important indicators; however, they don't tell the entire story. Today we know that libraries do more than just circulate materials. Libraries have become the "meeting place," a place where people of all ages can go to use a study room, attend a program, use the computer, and socialize. We also know that many people can easily access our collections and electronic resources from their home computers. So we must look beyond just the circulation statistics to determine the needs of our users and nonusers. In justifying the need for a bookmobile [at my former position], for instance, we looked "beyond" our walls and saw the need to reach the underserved in our community. We needed to provide library service to those populations— seniors, young children, new immigrants, and homebound—that could not easily get to a library building. We also looked at the growing residential development and saw a need to provide library service to areas at a distance from the current facilities. Building a new library structure was not an option at that time. We looked at the options and determined the best avenue would be a bookmobile.

It is important to know the demographics of our community. It is important to build a relationship with our schools and other community organizations. You want their support. Once you have your bookmobile, statistics are important to show the importance of this service and the need for continued support. The bookmobile's service to schools, senior facilities, neighborhoods, and community events resulted in circulation statistics that matched—and at times exceeded—the circulation of a small branch. Reaching the underserved also resulted in an increase in new library card registrations. The bookmobile offered the opportunity for many people to experience a library setting for the first time and to enjoy a welcoming, nonthreatening, fun library environment.

Q: Can you think of a specific time when this cooperation between schools and the public library has been beneficial to both parties?
A: The institution of the public library bookmobile was beneficial to both the public schools and the community as a whole. The teachers and the students had access to current fiction and nonfiction works that would support and enrich their leisure and educational reading. The public library's youth services and young adult librarians would visit the schools and booktalk titles found on the bookmobile and at the library buildings.

The bookmobile's collection was developed to meet the needs and demands of the general population and the leisure and curriculum needs of the school students. The collection offered students a wide variety of popular reading materials as well as subject areas that would reinforce their education. The collection had materials that would serve the diverse reading levels of the student population. Bilingual materials, high interest–low reading materials, classics, and current bestsellers were selected to reach the diverse student population. School media specialists could request materials for special projects from the public library or bookmobile or send assignment alerts to the public library or bookmobile. This communication allowed the public library to meet the research needs of the students. This type of cooperation also resulted in the public library's developing homework assistance for students. Special homework materials, such as dictionaries, textbooks, electronic databases, "live" homework help center, and other reference tools, were developed to assist students at all levels.

Q: If someone were working with an administrator who was not supportive, can you suggest ways to bring that administrator around?
A: Do your homework. Have all your facts, documentation, pros and cons, and community support gathered and ready to present to the administrator. Read the literature and have a good understanding of bookmobile service—or any program or service you wish to implement. Talk to people currently involved in the service. Again, gather data to support your views. Talk to community leaders and get their support. Look at the cost. Administrators may be supportive, but funding may be a problem. Look for grant opportunities. Present all your findings in a proposal to your administrator. The more information you can present, the better.

Let the principal know the purpose of the visit, which teachers were visited by the librarian, and how many students benefited from the visit. Also discuss how the visit assisted you in doing your job. For example, if you don't have an extensive historical fiction collection and the public library does, these visits and resource sharing help you save money in that area, so you can instead focus funding and time on building the collection to respond to the curriculum changes in science—where you have almost no titles. The public librarian's historical fiction booktalks expand the range of materials students have access to and free up your time to work with other students and teachers. Make a follow-up call to the public librarian to see which titles were popular, and double-check with the teachers to get an idea of which titles to purchase for your own collection.

Make sure the principal understands the process, time commitment, and effort involved in these collaborative endeavors. Keeping the lines of communication open might mean that your principal will think of you when he becomes aware of grant possibilities. Having a record of your activities on file will assist you when it comes to proposals—you have the statistics and information you need right at your fingertips. (See more on grants earlier in this chapter.)

The amount of information your administrator needs depends on the individual. As a school library media specialist in Kansas City, Missouri, said about public librarians visiting her school: "I did not have to convince the administrator, just get her to approve the schedule each year." In this case, the principal was comfortable with minimal information. You are the judge of your own situation. Cheryl Youse, the school library media specialist at Colquitt County High School in Moultrie, Georgia, said: "Honestly, I never even told the administration in advance. It was pretty much a non-issue. I just told the receptionist that we were having a guest from the public library and please direct them to the media center. I have never gotten any negative comments from administrators about any guests I have invited. Don't think I ever asked for permission either unless there was a fee involved or major disruption of the schedule would be required." Once again, understanding the climate you work in will make all the difference. Reporting requirements might also taper off over time, as your principal begins to trust your judgment.

As mentioned previously, keeping track of statistics is very important to the public library. Although it can be time consuming, you should check at least several times a year to get an indication of how your visits with the school, book bins/bags, registration nights, and summer reading programs are faring. Track these numbers over time. If you do booktalks, look at the circulation statistics for the materials you will be presenting, then check the numbers again two months, three months, and six months out. Compare similar titles that you haven't booktalked to estimate how book-talks impact the circulation of those materials. Information like this is valuable if your supervisor ever begins to doubt the wisdom of your forays outside the public library. If you receive cards or let-ters from students, share these with your supervisor and director. Make copies and see if they can be included in the monthly library board packet.

Work with your partner librarian on a presentation for both the school board and the public library board on the wonderful col-laborative projects you are doing together, *with the wonderful sup-port of your supervisors.* This is a great way to thank those in power for enabling you to do such an effective job. Supervisors should be rewarded for their support. Giving praise where praise is due helps grease the wheels for future endeavors.

Chapter 10

Keeping It Going

You have ideas, you have tools, and you have kept in regular contact with your colleague in the other library. You have progressed to the point where you are comfortable with each other, engage each other with projects and collaborations, jointly serve the needs of teachers and students, and consistently raise awareness of the importance of libraries. How do you keep this momentum going? The same old same old can become so routine over time that your partnership begins to feel like a chore rather than an exciting new possibility. And what happens to your collaborative efforts if your partner decides to take a new job across the state or across the country?

Any collaborative relationship encounters challenges. This connection, though, needs to endure, even long after you may have left your institution and even when you feel ready to scream as you put together your 200th teacher newsletter. Give yourself permission to scream, then try to come up with a new way of delivering information that will keep you engaged yet still do the job.

Moving Forward

As much as I love giving booktalks, there are days when I don't want to crack open a book. One year I spent 75 days in the schools, giving 375 booktalks. I couldn't read books fast enough to fill the need, and of course, once I booktalked a particular title, it was then checked out for months as students came in to read it. This was exactly the desired effect, but it made finding new material an interesting challenge. This effort kept me up late at night reading and listening to books on tape every day in the car. I'll say one thing for booktalks; they really make you examine your collection and pore over the new book carts!

As you can imagine, I got sick of my standard booktalk delivery and started branching out a bit. Instead of letting the students pick the order of the books I would talk about, I created cards with keywords related to the books. Students had to guess, simply by the cover and title, which book each card referred to. Sometimes I added a phrase or question to these cards, or sometimes I would call up students to help me act out a booktalk for Vivian Vande Velde's *Magic Can Be Murder*. (My booktalk involved naming several characters, and I didn't want students to get confused.) Students always loved it when I deviated from the norm. This also gave me the chance for a mental shake-up and to look at something I enjoyed in a slightly different way—just enough to revitalize myself.

Some people thrive on normalcy and the dependability of a routine. Others, myself included, tend to stagnate when things become too ordinary. Partnerships between libraries should be entered into with the idea that these relationships and structures will be in place for many years. As such, they may in time begin to grate on one or both parties. Try to assess whether your partner is someone who enjoys the constancy of an ongoing project or who likes to try something new every few years. Often, just a simple tweak can be enough to re-energize the most inert partner—especially if your partner is inactive due to boredom.

When launching any project, create a timeline. Include not only a targeted completion date but also whether the initiative will be repeated in the future if it has the desired outcomes. Build in a way to change the activity slightly from year to year, or establish a three-year cycle for reviewing ongoing plans. This gives you an opportunity to voice any concerns you might have down the road and to address problems that may have developed. Revisiting your arrangement helps keep the project fresh and gives you a chance to try something new. Some activities might be a one-time deal, and others might bear repeating every other year or every third year. In a school setting, the number of grades your school serves might dictate how often you should repeat a program. For example, in a K–6 building, you might want to do a given program every three years so that the kindergarten children have a chance to participate when they are young and again when they are older. In a high school setting, perhaps you will want to repeat a program only once every four years. Determine the goals and timetable of your project going in.

In this same vein, most libraries feel an obligation to do *something* for National Library Week. (If you work with teens, it might be Teen Read Week instead.) Many such events come up annually, so you might want to do a big push to advertise them only every few years. During the off years, you can still pay attention and promote the event, but you don't have to kill yourself every year, creating a new fantastic collaborative project that consumes you, your partner, and your valuable time for months. Large programs require vast amounts of time and energy, which are both in short supply at the best of times. Build in breaks for both of you to help keep things fresh and allow you time to revamp and reassess as necessary.

Over time, we all fight burnout, both in our own jobs and in collaborative undertakings with others. For many reasons, a given year might be more stressful for you than usual. School library media specialists might be dealing with teacher turnover as old friends retire and new, inexperienced teachers take their places. Or a new principal with a new agenda takes over the reins, placing new strains on your library. Public librarians are always faced with the possibility of changes in their schedule—or their very position. And budgetary concerns affect us all.

With collaboration, as with other aspects of your job, look outside your own situation to gain perspective and ideas. Even when I felt overwhelmed in my job as a public librarian, attending a conference, a system meeting, or a workshop always created new excitement in my job and gave me a new viewpoint. Seek out such events and opportunities to renew your own collaborative spirit. For example, Christine McNew, youth services consultant, Texas

State Library and Archives Commission, is in the process of creating an online course on school/public library cooperation with her colleague Naomi DiTullio in the Library Development Division. This course will initially be offered to Texas librarians; then the course creators will invite all state libraries to offer it for continuing education credit for school and public librarians throughout the U.S. Check for opportunities such as this in your own area.

Also, look around your system or state for groups that support school and public library collaboration. If a local group doesn't already exist, consider starting your own. That is what Jennifer Bromann, of Lincoln-Way Central High School in New Lenox, Illinois, did when she began her high school library media specialist position seven years ago (see sidebar on page 173).

Keep it fresh by making an effort not to overdo the programs you work on together, and try to establish at the outset whether each activity will be a one-shot deal or a continuing effort. Give yourself permission to say, "Let's try this, and if it doesn't work, we'll try something else," rather than repeating the same painfully bad project year after year. Seek outside advice and inspiration from others who are working to build the same types of relationships in a different city, county, or state. Last, don't be afraid to organize a support group yourself if you can't find one to meet the needs or goals you have for your partnerships.

For Posterity

How do you guarantee that all the hard work and sweat equity you and your collaborative partner have put into this balanced and important relationship will survive after a specific project has ended or when the priorities of the organizations you work for change? How can you influence your supervisor or your colleagues to establish a framework for long-term collaboration? This situation differs for everyone. Think about the following circumstances, and determine which might be applicable to you.

Vertical Teamwork with Libraries Too

Jennifer Bromann, library department chair, Lincoln-Way Central High School, New Lenox, Illinois.

When I worked in a public library, we met bimonthly with other area librarians to share ideas, hear speakers, and ask questions. One question that I always had was if we could invite school librarians to our meetings. I was always told no, school librarians can't get out of the building. I thought that we could at least ask them, because maybe they would like to attend—but I was always shot down. Then I *became* a school librarian and learned that the rumor was partly true. There are not as many opportunities to attend conferences, and it is more important that I am at my school to assist students— but we definitely can get away for the occasional meeting.

I missed the exchange of ideas between my peers. Then, when I attended school meetings to discuss our vertical team program, I thought that the [public] library should be included too. The concept behind a vertical team is to align your curriculum with those of all grade levels within the same discipline. For example, high school English teachers would meet with the junior high teachers to make sure that books or topics weren't being duplicated or over- or underemphasized. But more important, a vertical team is meant to reinforce skills through the years. By senior year, students should be hearing the same terminology in an English class (or any other discipline) that they heard way back in sixth grade, or even earlier. Skills are layered so that they learn a concept, but keep building on that concept or progressively apply the skills to gradually more difficult work.

Although this concept can be defined and used in various ways, our school adapted the model by the College Board, which defines *vertical team* as "a group of teachers from different grade levels in given disciplines, who work to develop and implement a vertically-aligned program to help students acquire the skills and knowledge for success in the AP Program." We thought that we could take this concept and adapt it to work with all of the libraries in the area. We not only invited the high schools, but the junior highs, elementary schools, public libraries, library systems, and even the junior college in the area. Even though we are not a traditional vertical team, we decided that the name still best fit our needs, so we call ourselves the Lincoln-Way Area Library Vertical Team.

The meetings are held twice a year and attract 10–25 attendees who work with all age levels and library types. The public libraries often send representatives from their children's, young adult, and reference departments, since all of these areas work with children and/or teenagers, and even some public library directors attend. School media centers send the person responsible for each building or a representative from all the schools in their district. We try to vary the locations, but meetings have traditionally been held at the high schools or at the public libraries. We found that having the meetings at 12:30 PM worked best, because media specialists could attend part of the meeting on their lunch breaks or did not have to worry about returning to work, since meetings typically last until 2:30 or 3:00 PM. The hosting libraries either provide lunch or collect a small donation of between $3 and $5 for lunch. Meetings could also be held after school, on common institute days, on early release dates, or on other dates designated for vertical team meetings if all the subject areas and schools in your district participate.

We began by creating a list of all the schools and libraries that fed into our high school district, including the two library systems that work with some of our different schools. At the beginning of the year, one of our library staff members would call all the schools to get updated names, email addresses, and phone numbers. If you have limited staff, you could recruit help from one of the other schools or libraries in the area to get things started. Now that I have an email distribution list, I send out messages asking for meeting dates that work best for everyone. If the date is planned far enough in advance, people can usually adapt their schedule to this meeting.

I also ask for suggestions for possible discussion topics, which change at each meeting. Typical content has included programming, overdue books, curriculum, weeding or deselection, terminology, and databases. At our last meeting we also invited school and public library administrators to discuss common concerns. Recently, we decided to add an article to read and discuss and a topic for book sharing. These articles usually relate to one of the topics we are discussing and are selected by a different team member each time, while the topics for book sharing have included reference books, boy books, multicultural books, and professional resources. We then conclude each meeting with a discussion about the date, location, and topics for the next meeting. One of our future goals is to establish a shared research/information literacy model that can be used by all of the schools. We tried to establish a common curriculum for each age level, but one school district already had such a curriculum, which we borrowed and shared as a starting point.

I usually run the meetings by calling on people to speak and announcing the topics we will be discussing. However, this can be shared or assigned to the library hosting the meeting or to a different librarian or media specialist each time. It can be a bit time consuming for one person, so the information does not always get out in a timely manner, depending on how busy the school year has become. To keep these meetings running smoothly, we need to update our mailing list, email members for possible dates, determine the best date, create an invitation, mail and email the invitation, email for topic suggestions, create an agenda, determine an article, order lunch, and prepare the minutes or a summary of the meeting. Many of these tasks can be shared if there are people willing or able to assist.

These meetings have been beneficial to me and to others in many ways. Although our main goal is to develop and implement a common curriculum and information literacy model, we gain much more. We get to know the people who have previously worked with our students, who will work with our students, or who are currently working with our students in the public libraries. It is easier to communicate on the phone or through email when you know the people to whom you are talking. We feel comfort in knowing that others are dealing with the same issues we face. And we get to share ideas and ask others how they handle specific situations. Although the preparation for these meetings can take time from an already busy schedule, these opportunities to meet with one another have become an essential part of our year.

First, start with yourself. Build the collaborative process into your yearly goals. Most supervisors encourage their employees to be forward thinkers, to set personal objectives, and to determine how each will be met. Use this opportunity to focus on your collaboration and show how determined you are to continue this endeavor with the other library. Having goals and objectives in black and white each year will keep them front and center for you and your immediate supervisor and will also show your administration how valuable this relationship is to you and your library. A school library media specialist, for instance, might include some of the following in her yearly goals:

- Contact the public librarian monthly to keep abreast of current events at the public library that could benefit students and teachers. Display relevant posters or flyers in the school library media center.

- Follow up on last year's collaborative effort to see if you can continue it during the next school year. Make adjustments as needed.

- Invite the public librarian to your district's school library media specialist meetings.

- Engage the public librarian in creating a joint book discussion group, with meetings alternating between the school library media center and the public library.

A public librarian can consider some of these yearly goals:

- Establish or maintain contact with the school library media specialist in each school you serve.

- Hold a meeting with the school library media specialists in your district to determine the curricular needs of their students and teachers. Evaluate the public library collection to see where you might add materials to supplement the resources of the school libraries.

- Plan at least one joint program this year. It can be an author visit or a presentation relating to a curriculum unit, such as biomes, mammals, or slavery.

- Booktalk or present to students in each school at least once this year.

While these ideas are not new, it is helpful to get them in writing so you can review your goals and keep them in your sights if you need extra momentum to maintain your involvement with the other library. Making your plans known to your administration only assists you in the long run.

Many libraries and schools are investing serious time and energy into the creation of long-range plans, typically in five-year cycles. Create your own five-year plan for partnership and collaboration. Concentrate on how you want to see your relationship progress over time, and sit down with your counterpart to get ideas on how each of you would like to proceed. Of course, like any long-range plan, your plan needs to be flexible enough to expand and transform as you grow more comfortable with each other and see additional possibilities for your relationship.

Start small. Perhaps your goal for year one could be that you each attend the other's important meetings. Year two's goal could be for the school library media specialist to host a tea for teachers at the public library. At this event, the collaborating librarians would explain in detail how they work together to better serve the needs of students and teachers. Year three could focus on strengthening the ties between the public library and the school through curriculum mapping and identifying two or more programs the public library and school could sponsor jointly. Year four might target a specific audience, such as a grade level, for a themed unit, with both libraries contributing time and resources. Year five could see the two librarians targeting a need shared by both libraries and working together to find a grant that would support their work with an identified group for the greater good of the community of learners. Obviously, your five-year plan will vary, depending on the needs you see in the population you serve. Sit down and discuss your ideas. Set up timelines, objectives, and assessments of success to give you a greater understanding of each other as well as a clear roadmap to follow in the coming years.

Public librarians can work with their administration to create a shared-services agreement with certain schools or entire school districts. A formal agreement is a good way to achieve stability and gain official recognition of your working relationship. Deborah Motley, a young adult services librarian for Orion Township Public Library in Lake Orion, Michigan, reports that this arrangement has worked well for her area: "Our library has entered into a formal agreement with the local school district that allows us to go to registrations, parent-teacher conferences, and any other events where there are lots of students and parents, to give out card applications, flyers on homework help, and anything else we think is useful. I've spoken to the district's media specialists about some collaborative efforts, and I've attended staff meetings to let teachers know about our live homework help and my availability to booktalk. The biggest piece however, is that we have set up a system where any school personnel can request books from the library and we'll have them delivered to the school. This is to supplement what is in the media centers. This has been a very successful collaboration."

Spelling out your agreement helps you focus your efforts and gives you a chance to evaluate what kinds of services are needed. It also creates a perfect opportunity for public librarians to work directly with school library media specialists to establish each of their library's needs, while giving the public library access to the population school librarians serve. Clearly, an agreement such as this can be reached only with the support of both the public library and the school district's administration, and this more formal option might not work for everyone. This could be a goal you work toward attaining in the future.

Many public libraries are seeing the need for a staff position that focuses on collaborating, assisting, and serving the schools in their area, thus demonstrating the value these libraries place on such involvement. If your public library currently does not have a school liaison, try incorporating association and participation with the schools into your own job description. This will help keep it front and center if you ever leave your job.

When Someone Leaves

As the saying goes, "All good things must come to an end." In any professional relationship, one or the other of you is bound to leave, for any of a variety of reasons: new employment opportunity, retirement, relocation, or perhaps even a change of profession. For some this will be a chance to stir the pot and get some new ideas cooking; for others, it truly spells the loss of a good friend. Leaving my position as a young adult librarian was difficult for me because I truly loved my vocation and the people I worked with on a daily basis. I left not only my colleagues in the two public library buildings in my district but also the teachers and school library media specialists at four middle schools and two high schools. While we all tend to feel that we're irreplaceable, it can also be good for our library to hire someone with a fresh perspective and new ideas. Leaving can be hard to do, but it offers everyone a chance to grow.

You Leave

So you have made the decision to leave your current job, for whatever reason. However, you want to make sure the time and energy you have invested with the other library doesn't get thrown out with all your old papers. What can you do to ensure the survival of your labors? This is one reason to make an effort to incorporate collaboration into your job description: It increases the chances your employer will seek a replacement who is open to participation in these types of relationships. Before you leave, you can help smooth the transition for this new person.

Create a binder with all the information about your transactions with the other library (or libraries). This can be a quick run-down of the programs you worked on and what they involved, and it might just mean making a copy of some items and information from your files. Departing public librarians might include:

- Contact information for each school library media specialist in your district, and the names of the schools your library serves. Include phone numbers, email addresses, and any other pertinent information—such as the projects you have done with each school and whether they were successful.

- The established procedures for promoting programs in the schools. Do you have to get the superintendent and/or principal's permission for each promotion, or can you fax PR materials directly to the individual schools?

- A list of the school library media specialists who use public library services extensively. What do they tend to need on a yearly basis? Do they like to have books pulled and put on reserve in the public library for class projects? Arrange class visits to the library? Schedule booktalks?

- A list of any projects in the pipeline, and ideas for possible future projects.

- Samples of ongoing communication with the schools, such as newsletters. Explain how often these go out and to whom they are sent.

- Specifics on summer reading promotion. How does each school handle visits? Does one school hold a large assembly, but two others like librarians to visit individual classes? Does yet another school prefer to schedule class visits in the school library media center?

It may take some time to compile this information if you have extensive dealings with the schools. It will be invaluable, though, to the person taking over your position. An overview of your school partnership gives the new person a chance to decide how to proceed, with a clear understanding of what has gone on before.

If you are leaving a school library media center, create a similar binder for your replacement. While it will be hard to find the time to put this together, since you have a whole library to get ready for the new person, it might be even more imperative here than in a public library. Many public librarians are conditioned to consider working with the schools, but school library media specialists often do not have that same perspective. Let the new school librarian know how important your interaction with the local public library is for the well-being of students and teachers in the school. Emphasize the value of fostering ongoing positive relations between the two libraries. Consider adding this information to your binder:

- The name and hours of the local public library (or libraries) you work with. Include information about the students in your school, and explain that because of boundary issues, students may be in different public library districts.

- Contact information for individuals at the public library who have assisted you in the past. If possible, include their schedules since most public librarians work non-standard hours.

- A list of some services the public library or libraries provide to schools, such as providing teacher cards, pulling books, loaning books to the school library, and giving booktalks.

- A list of the public library programs you have promoted in the past.

- A list of any shared resources, from meeting rooms to databases.

- A list of the teachers in your building who regularly utilize the public library, and the services they use.

- Information on summer reading promotion. List the steps that must be taken internally each year in order for the public library to promote summer reading in your school. Highlight efforts that have been the most successful.

- Information on ongoing partnerships and collaborations with the public library, and ideas for future possibilities.

When leaving any job, you are likely to be anxious. Keep in mind that starting a new job is equally stressful, so anything you can do to assist the person taking over your position will help ensure the continuation of the services you have already established—and will allow for future growth.

New Beginnings

An interview with Randi Carreno, young adult librarian, Fountaindale Public Library District, Bolingbrook, Illinois.

Q: How did your position evolve into what it is today?
A: Well, I was first hired as a reference librarian in the Information Services Department, and another candidate was hired as the young adult librarian. That candidate didn't work out, so I was asked to make the transition to YA librarian at Romeoville (one of two libraries in our district). I found it a little difficult in the beginning—I had taken a couple of courses, but my library experience up to that point had been in the children's department and reference desk of a small library, one year at an academic library, and then about three months at Fountaindale. This was my first professional job, and I was really very nervous about getting everything right.

Q: How did you begin partnering in new ways with the schools?
A: I just started emailing the school media specialists, and I have worked most closely with one who calls or emails whenever he needs something—I work really hard to accommodate him in anything he needs. I do have contact with some of the other schools, mainly two middle schools and both of the high schools. I am trying to make myself as available as possible.

Q: What are some of the projects you have done as a result of these partnerships?
A: I have attended career fairs and open houses, collaborated on author visits, given presentations on library databases, dropped off summer newsletters, talked about the summer reading program and the FRANK volunteer program (which is for teens to volunteer and assist the Children's Department with summer reading), and coordinated library visits. We have had several walking field trips to the library, where I

gave booktalks, assisted students with author projects, and more. I am working with an English teacher to plan a Young Writer's Conference, in which students will be coming to the library for workshops and to hear an author speak. I booked this author for their visit.

I have worked with one school library media specialist to bring in three teen authors this year. We had Lesléa Newman in the fall, and Angela Johnson and Doug Wilhelm in the spring. This school library media specialist was awarded a grant that allowed him to bring in authors during the school year; he initially booked the authors, and we piggybacked on him, which let us bring them in at a reduced rate. We shared the responsibility for the authors' transportation.

Q: Has your partnering gone beyond individual schools?
A: I have been working with the curriculum coordinators for the Valley View School District as well. We started by displaying proposed textbooks and novel lists for parent approval, as part of the curriculum adoption process. From there, I have been working with the high school coordinator and the middle school coordinator, acquiring textbooks and getting the updated textbook list for the library. I was also asked to help create a summer reading list for the high school AP students.

Q: Any advice for librarians facing a new position that might allow them to collaborate with the schools?
A: My advice for new librarians would be: Don't be afraid. Use the school library media specialists! They have been so instrumental in promoting my programs and keeping me current with events and assignments. If your department or management staff forgets that school services *are* important, just keep bugging them. I just keep working at it—asking to go to events, asking to go to schools and to ride on the bookmobile. There is still so much more I would like to do with the schools.

Before you officially leave, make sure your counterpart in the other library knows when you will be going. After all, you don't want that person to find out by calling the library and unexpectedly meeting the new person on the phone. This is simply a matter of respect. If you have partnership commitments lined up after you are scheduled to leave, make arrangements for someone else to cover these responsibilities. If you have time, sit down with the other librarian and brainstorm ways to keep services flowing smoothly during the transitional period. Consider the teachers as well. Let them know whom to contact about public library services if the replacement school librarian isn't able to focus on connecting with the public library right away—or if it takes some time to hire a replacement. Public librarians should make sure the teachers they have worked with know when to expect a replacement. Let them know that you cannot be certain the new person will offer exactly the same services. She might be terrified of giving booktalks, while you loved them—but might instead be fantastic at getting big-name authors to visit. Just because someone is different doesn't mean she isn't valuable in serving student and teacher needs.

You Are Left

When you are the one left behind, you might be thrilled by the prospect of working with someone new, or you might feel abandoned, or you might simply be ready to get down to business with a new colleague. It all depends on the relationship you had with the person who is leaving. In any event, view this as a chance to create new connections or improve on those already established between your libraries. Realize that the administration's attitudes might also affect the new person's attitude. As Debbie Allen, an elementary school librarian in Starkville, Mississippi, states: "The public library director is very supportive; I know that not all public library officials are eager to collaborate, so I would not assume that new personnel would make this a priority." Once again, knowing the culture is important. Even if you don't agree with the values of a particular library or administrator, seek ways to continue collab-oration and to help the new person see its value.

Acknowledging differences up front may be the best approach to working with a new colleague. Betty Brennan, a high school library media specialist and national-board-certified teacher in Seattle, Washington, comments: "Yes, it does change, but I just start with a new person and we work on open communication." Starting fresh may require you to go back to the beginning. As Brennan says, get those communication lines in place first. It might be frustrating to have to start a new relationship—but you did it before, and you can do it again.

When you do begin to work with the new librarian, keep in mind that he might be a bit overwhelmed while adjusting to the new position. Ask if there is any way you can assist in your areas of overlapping services. Try to avoid comparisons to the previous librarian, whether good or bad. Each librarian has his own ideas on how best to serve his library's population—and what seems like a crazy idea at first just might prove genius after all. As with any relationship, give it time to grow, while nurturing it along. Don't be afraid to start small again and gradually rebuild.

What It Comes Down To

In the end, it all comes down to dedication and a willingness to expand your horizons by reaching out to one another. Of course we all focus on the most valuable uses of our time, whether it be keeping current with journals, lists, and blogs; working with stu-dents and teachers; developing the collection; or any other important parts of running and working in a library. However, if you personally do not believe in the value of collaboration, it will not happen. It starts with your recognizing the importance of collaboration between libraries and creating a plan to act accordingly. School and public libraries can grow closer and become intertwined only when the people working in these libraries consciously decide that working together is central to both libraries' values and goals. As we all know about a relationship, when it's good, it's good, and when it's great ... it's *magic!*

Recommended Reading

Achterman, D. (2006). Beyond Wikipedia. *Teacher Librarian, 34*(2), 19–22.

Baxter, K., & Haggberg, S. (2000). Ladies who lunch: Despite their Minnesota guilt, a school and public librarian get to know each other. *School Library Journal, 46*(9), 33.

Baxter, K., & Kochel, M. (1999). *Gotcha!: Nonfiction booktalks to get kids excited about reading.* Westport, CT: Libraries Unlimited.

Braun, L. (2007). *Listen up! Podcasting for schools and libraries.* Medford, NJ: Information Today, Inc.

Brewer, S., & Milam, P. (2006). SLJ's technology survey: 2006. *School Library Journal, 52*(6), 46–50.

Bromann, J. (1999). The toughest audience on earth. *School Library Journal, 45*(10), 60–62.

Bromann, J. (2001). *Booktalking that works.* New York: Neal-Schuman Publishers.

Bundy, A., & Amey, L. (2006). Libraries like no others: Evaluating the performance and progress of joint use libraries. *Library Trends, 54*(4), 501–518.

Bush, G. (2003). *The school buddy system: The practice of collaboration.* Chicago: American Library Association.

Bush, G. (2006). Walking the road between libraries: Best practices in school and public library cooperative activities. *School Library Media Activities Monthly, 22*(6), 25–28.

Farkas, M. (2007). *Social software in libraries: Building collaboration, communication and community online.* Medford, NJ: Information Today, Inc.

Fitzgibbons, S. (2001). School and public library relationships: Déjà vu or new beginnings. *Journal of Youth Services in Libraries, 14*(3), 3–7.

Gerding, S., & MacKellar, P. (2006). *Grants for libraries: A how-to-do-it manual and CD-ROM for librarians.* New York: Neal-Schuman.

Gniewek, D. (2000). The rotating library. *School Library Journal, 46*(8), 35.

Guevara, A., & Sexton, J. (2000). Extreme booktalking: YA booktalkers reach 6,000 students each semester! *Voice of Youth Advocates, 23*(2), 98–101.

Hastings, J. (2005). Cool tools: A savvy librarian reports on promising technology. *School Library Journal, 51*(9), 42–45.

Hauser, J. (2007). Media specialists can learn Web 2.0 tools to make schools more cool. *Computers in Libraries, 27*(2), 6–8 continued 47–48.

John, L. (2006). *Running book discussion groups: A how-to-do-it manual for librarians.* New York: Neal Shuman.

Jones, J. (2004). Come together. *School Library Journal, 50*(3), 45.

Jones, P., & Shoemaker, J. (2001). *Do it right: Best practices for serving young adults in school and public libraries.* New York: Neal-Schuman.

Knowles, E., & Smith, M. (2003). *Talk about books!: A guide for book clubs, literature circles, and discussion groups, grades 4-8.* Westport, CT: Libraries Unlimited.

Mediavilla, C. (2001). Why library homework centers extend society's safety net. *American Libraries, 32*(11), 40–42.

Park, C. (2005) Joint use libraries: Are they worth the challenges? *Texas Library Journal, 81*(1), 6–10.

Pawlas, G. (2005). *The administrator's guide to school community relations* (2nd ed.). Larchmont, NY: Eye on Education.

Peck, P. (2003). The big event. *School Library Journal, 49*(3), 45.

Ryan, S. (2001). "Be nice to the secretary" and other ways to work successfully with schools. *Journal of Youth Services in Libraries, 14*(3), 15–17.

Singer, R. (1999). School-age children and the public library. *Journal of Youth Services in Libraries, 13*(1), 36–41.

Slezak, E. (2000). *The book group book: A thoughtful guide to forming and enjoying a stimulating book discussion group* (3rd ed.). Chicago: Chicago Review Press.

Snyder, T. (2000). *Getting lead-bottomed administrators excited about school library media centers.* Westport, CT: Libraries Unlimited.

Tice, M. (2001). Queens Borough Public Library and the connecting libraries and schools project. *Journal of Youth Services in Libraries, 14*(3), 11–13.

Tucey, R., & Rooney, C. (1999). The school/public library alliance: The Pueblo Library District experience. *Colorado Libraries 25*(1), 21–24.

Van Linden Tol, P., Vasquez, C., & Westover, S. (2005). Reaching out to middle and high schools. *Public Libraries, 44*(2), 65–66, 85.

York, S. (2008). *Booktalking authentic multicultural literature: Fiction, history, and memoirs for teens.* Columbus, OH: Linworth.

Ziarnik, N. R. (2003). *School & public libraries: Developing the natural alliance.* Chicago: American Library Association.

About the Author

Tasha Squires currently works as a young adult consultant for the Shorewood-Troy Public Library District in Shorewood, Illinois, collaborating on programs for teens while completing her certification as a school library media specialist. Previously, she was the young adult librarian for the Fountaindale Public Library District in Bolingbrook, Illinois, for more than eight years. During her tenure there, she worked extensively with the public school district and made wonderful connections with the teachers, students, and administrators.

Tasha has presented throughout northern Illinois and at the Illinois Library Association's annual conference on topics such as teen award winners, booktalking for middle school students, and collaborating with schools to serve young adults. She has contributed articles to *Know Kidding: The Best of the Best in Youth Services* (Wheeling, Illinois, 2003), and the *Info Career Trends* electronic newsletter. She is looking forward to beginning her new career as a school library media specialist. Tasha holds an MLIS from Dominican University.

Index